Praise for
Romancing the Loan!

The book is wonderful, (it) really is something of benefit to business owners; but more than a book about business and how to deal with banks, (it's) a great book about how to improve your life.
   Carlos Evans, Senior Bank Officer

"Relationship economics" is the term that Larry Tyler has offered in helping bridge the gap between those business men and women who state that family is their most important relationship contrasted with the actual time being spent on family relationships being quite low. Using personal relationships as a metaphor throughout Romancing the Loan, Larry is able to creatively apply many of those principles to the banking industry. I found it refreshing when he asked a person seeking a loan to imagine the wants and needs of the banker with whom this individual was about to make a presentation. In another section he asks the reader to consider a role-reversal and to be in the place of the lender. It includes actual case studies by the author and not just the theory from a textbook. I enjoyed your blend of quotes, personal stories, bulleted suggestions and the use of metaphors all the way through your book.
   Daniel Eckstein, Ph.D., Professor of Medical Psychology, Saba University School of Medicine, Saba, Dutch-Antilles, West Indies. Author, *Leadership by Encouragement, Psychological Fingerprints, and Raising Respectful Kids in a Rude World.* www.leadershipbyencouragement.com

I'm really excited about your book and what it has to offer business owners and entrepreneurs. You have managed to make what I expected to be a dry subject VERY interesting. Your book is good to the last word! Bravo! I'm motivated. People need this book.

Beverly Lewis, nationally recognized speaker, trainer, success coach and entrepreneur. http://lifepointspeaker.com/

Without an ethical foundation on the part of borrowers and lenders alike, there can be no sustainable financial system. People cannot merely have good intentions and want to be successful; they must possess the basic tools to become successful. Your book will assist others in their quest to support themselves, their families and communities in a great thing.

Louis E. Buck, Jr., Ph.D. Wesley Elingburg Distinguished Professor of Business Innovation, Director, Center for Entrepreneurship & Innovation, College of Business, Western Carolina University

Your philosophy about building a relationship with your banker is worth gold! What a remarkable book! "Romancing the Loan" provides invaluable guidance on everything you need to know about obtaining a business loan; from building a relationship with your lender, building your credit, creating value, making the right networking connections, repositioning your business during tough times, understanding lending rules and laws, developing a success mindset and being willing to be coached by people that have "walked the walk." Bravo!

Ken Marsh, CEO Fearless Networking ,Keynote Speaker, Trainer, Curriculum Developer and author of *Fearless Networking*-2nd ed. http://www.fearlessnetworkers.com/

ROMANCING
THE
LOAN

14 PRINCIPLES FOR OPENING
YOUR LENDER'S VAULT

Larry Tyler

Alpine Publishing
The Mind at a Higher Elevation

"Romancing the Loan"
14 Principles of Opening Your Lender's Vault

Alpine Publishing Company
1281 Georgia Rd. #374
Franklin, NC 28734
E-mail: larry@upyourbusines.biz

ISBN: 978-0-9827996-0-4
Printed in the U.S.A.

Cover, Interior Design and Edit by V. Dawn Mast

Contents

Chapter   **Page**

Acknowledgements

This is a simple book about a very important subject addressed to some of the world's most important people, small to mid-size business owners, on obtaining capital with which businesses can operate, subsist and thrive. This book would never have come into existence without the help of thousands of business owners with whom I've had the pleasure of working during my 37 year lending career. Being able to test ideas and theories in the crucible of actual experience was thrilling, enlightening and gratifying. I ventured through almost four decades of different fiscal and monetary policies, several recessions and several economic booms. Life as a business lender was never boring and always very challenging.

To Jim Gallien, a Houston CPA who was the best at his trade I ever had the opportunity to work with: Thanks for the many hours of your personal time answering accounting questions and coaching me on financial shenanigans.

To Steve Hansen, CPA, entrepreneurship professor, entrepreneur and asset–based lending and factoring guru. Thanks for your like-minded and like-hearted friendship and the opportunity to speak to a number of your classes satisfying my "itch" to share what I've learned through the 'school of hard knocks'.

Thanks to God for the leading, direction, wisdom and words for this book. I am so grateful for His guidance into what I feel is an integral truth for us all at this time, the value and importance of ***romancing relationships.***

My special thanks and love goes to Vickie, my wife, best friend and fellow adventurer. Your help via suggestions, brain storming ideas, editing, support and encouragement all during this project was incredible. You put your own book and projects on hold to help me not only with this book but the transition of my career from a business lender to a business advisor, coach, speaker and author. This venture was truly a team effort and one worth modeling to others. It is one thing to write about romance and relationships, but it is quite another to live it. I stumble often in walking my talk but through our relationship I realize learning about romance and unconditional love is an ongoing class in the school of life and relationships. Vickie, your modeling of both unconditional love and romance is a constant source of inspiration and strength.

Foreword

You have a remarkable and incredibly insightful book in your hands right now. Larry Tyler shares with you the secrets to, as he says, "open the vault with your lender". He takes you into the mind and heart of your lender/banker so you dramatically increase the likelihood of getting the money you need to grow your business and create the company of your dreams.

I am a voracious reader of business books and I have never seen anyone take on this subject better than Larry has. He weaves the human aspects of romance and love into how to approach your lender and build a strong, trusting relationship with them. He helps you see and understand the human side of the person you will be asking to loan you money. So simple but brilliant at the same time. We all forget to look at the people we do business with as humans with their own view of life, their own worries, their own dreams, and their own way of making decisions. In fact, I am going to start looking at all my business relationships differently from now on. And I bet you will too after you read this book.

I have been a CPA for over 27 years now. The majority of that time was in Chief Financial Officer (CFO) roles and as a consultant to entrepreneurs. I realized early in my career I had a special understanding of the mind of the entrepreneur and I had a special talent for helping them better understand and relate to the financial side of their business. I always knew it was a special insight that existed because I took the time to really understand how they think and how they view the world. One of their limitations was linking their vision and strategy into financial performance and helping them see how a strong accounting and finance function was central to their success. So I built a niche helping them in that side of the business while always making sure they fully understood how it was helping them grow the company and make more money.

This book does something similar because Larry was a banker himself for over 30 years. And he has opened himself up to share with you exactly how the banker thinks and makes decisions about your loan proposal. What an advantage that creates for you. It's almost like giving you the keys to the vault.

The book shows you how to get connected to your lender and stay connected. He teaches you how to speak their language and why that is so important to receiving the keys to the vault.

Larry also reinforces a message near and dear to my heart. That you have to have good numbers and good cash flow projections when you talk to your banker. There is no telling how many loan proposals are shot down every single day because the business owner tried to wing it with their numbers. A lender will send you packing if they see you don't have a good handle on the financial side of your business or if you have financial and cash flow projections that have not been well thought out.

When I wrote my first book, *Never Run Out of Cash: The 10 Cash Flow Rules You Can't Afford to Ignore,* my primary goal was to help business owners and entrepreneurs take control of their cash flow. I had seen so many businesses get in trouble because they didn't understand just a few, simple principles that could have made all the difference for them. And one of the biggest mistakes people make is thinking they can run a business without cash flow projections. It's like driving on the freeway in a rainstorm without turning on your windshield wipers: You can't see the cars in front of you or behind you; you're just hoping the rain stops before you end up in a terrible accident. Cash flow projections provide you the visibility you need to make smarter and more profitable business decisions.

Larry shows you how important cash flow projections are to your lender. He gives you a peek inside their brain so you can understand how they use them and how you have to be prepared to show them that you know exactly what's going on with the cash flow of your business.

Follow Larry's step-by-step process and you will develop a strong relationship with your lender that will pay dividends for you long into the future.

I know you will benefit from reading this book the same way I have. I have already started using the principles and I am excited about the results.

Philip Campbell,
Consultant and author of *Never Run Out of Cash: The 10 Cash Flow Rules You Can't Afford to Ignore.*
www.Never RunOutOfCash.com

Romancing the Loan

Preface

Legacy of the Loan-A-Ranger Is Renewed

> *You win games on your strengths not on your weaknesses*   Bear Bryant

It was a beautiful but chilly evening in the late spring of 2009. Steve, the CEO of a small local business, and I had just met to go over the details of what he had experienced in the previous three days.   He had just signed the papers on three separate loan transactions that generated a net decrease of $6,000 per month in cash outflow from his business. Signing the documents resulted in everything he wanted and needed which, after careful scrutiny and analysis, would help preserve his company during this recession and prepare the company for stronger financial footing when the local business fortunes changed for the positive.

We sat on the patio of the restaurant to toast the occasion. Steve was thrilled and so proud to have closed the deals that greatly reduced his cash outflow and would make so much difference for the company as well as for his and the families of all of his employees. The sense of relief showed on his face and in his eyes that the ordeal with his lenders was finally done. About 90 days prior he didn't think things were going to work out at all.

After our toast, we reflected on the past several years that led up to this huge occasion.

His story leads to another story - mine...How the Legacy of the Loan-A-Ranger was renewed.

We had met when I first moved to the small mountain community several years earlier. In order to connect with business owners of the community I had joined several associations. Steve was in more than one of these and we gradually became friends. We were sitting together after one of the meetings and I asked Steve the history of his business.

Steve had been in business over twenty years and it had been an uphill climb until about seven years ago. Starting in 2002 his hard work, perseverance and networking with the right people started to pay off. Annual profits began to increase, word of his knowledge and business was spreading and people were calling to do business with him from the surrounding states.

As his relationships with local bankers improved, Steve increased his borrowing, put his profits in local real estate investments and diversified his asset holdings. Economic times were good in the area; there were more banks than possible loan or deposit customers, and lending requirements were lax. As an honest business man with strong ties and commitment to the local community, an excellent payment history and a sound business that easily cash flowed all debts, he was a wanted borrower by all the local banks. Steve had always been extremely mindful of interest rates and because he was a 'prime borrower', he usually got the lowest rates offered by each lender in the community.

Steve noticed in late 2007 the signs of some economic shifts and his intuition told him this economic downshift might last for several years. He began to tighten his belt on expenses, looking for ways to reduce or cut unnecessary spending and ways to increase profit and top line revenues. His major strategy was to stockpile cash.

One day in early 2009 I received a call from Steve. He explained briefly his view of the current economic situation and said he wanted to visit with me about his business and possibly engage me to help him with several pending loan situations. We scheduled a meeting for the next day.

After a friendly greeting the next words out of his mouth were, **"I don't know what I'm going to do!"**

Steve spent the next hour explaining his dilemma while I listened and took notes, occasionally asking a clarifying question. I could tell several things were bothering him, aside from his current business issues. Reaching into his pocket and pulling out a small pill case, he confessed to suddenly getting severe headaches, one of which he was currently experiencing and having stomach pains like acid reflux on a frequent basis, which he had never had before. He admitted,

"I believe the stress and anxiety of this economic climate and having to confront bankers is affecting my health."

Money was very tight even though he had stockpiled cash the past year. While business was active, top line revenues were down by a fourth. He had just determined several moves he made years ago to increase revenues and profit were losing money and, by trying to help others in the community, he was grossly overstaffed.

After listening to his story, I agreed to help him and suggested we go back to his office so I could get copies of financials, tax returns and several other items I needed to properly review his current and overall financial picture. As we were pulling some financial data, he outlined what he was planning and what he wanted me to do for him. He had several sizeable real estate loans on which he was hoping the banks would reduce his payments and one large loan that was maturing soon. He told me the bank with the maturing loan refused to renew the loan for more than one year. Steve's goal was to move the loan to another bank and seek a three or five year loan. He feared the country was facing a period of years with hyperinflation and since loan rates would likely skyrocket, now was the time to lock in a low rate in order to keep his cash outflow at a minimum until the economy improved.

Part of his plan was for me to put the financial data into a format the bankers might want and then he would take the information to the various banks. I asked him if I could ask some questions – which he agreed to:

- What type of reception or reaction do you feel you will receive to your requests from the banks?
- Do you know the current mood of the bankers?
- What is the current financial position of each bank you will be visiting? The bank's current financial status or rating might determine their response to your requests.
- Do you have all the data the bank might want or need to help them make a decision?
- Have you thought through what questions the bankers might ask and what your answers will be?

- Do you know what paperwork the banker might have to prepare, based on your requests, and how you can help make the banker's job easier?
- Are you prepared to pay fees to the bank as a result of a favorable response to your request?
- Have you thought about where the minds of the bankers might go when you tell them your problems?

Steve thought about these questions for a few minutes and then somewhat defensively said, **"You'd think I was being prepped to be a witness in a court trial!"**

I grinned at him and said, "You're correct, you will be on trial and this is life and death to your business, so let's get to work."

He responded, "I never thought about approaching bankers in this manner, but I guess you are right, it IS life and death, so let's get after it".

I told him I would call him in a day or so to see if he'd found the other financials and data I would need to properly put together a loan presentation and modification requests on the other loans.

At this point my mind took a quick imaginary trip and I saw myself sitting on an old porch with the retired Lone Ranger absorbing the wisdom he had gained in his years of rescuing people in distress. It occurred to me these were new times and

business owners don't need *rescuing*, they need *empowering*!

Returning to reality, I knew what I had to do in the ensuing years... help business owners who, although quite knowledgeable about their business and industry, needed

someone to help relieve the pain and stress of dealing with lenders and to help bring peace of mind back to their businesses and lives.

Several days later when I met with Steve I could tell he was approaching this task with a much different mindset than when we first met. I was optimistic we were headed in the correct direction but knew how he handled my list of suggestions would determine his success with the bankers.

As we delved into the questions and how to best present his case before each individual lender, I quickly saw more changes in his thinking would be necessary. Because of the many years of being in a very competitive banking situation, good economic times and Steve's reputation as a good and honest businessman, he wasn't required to provide the local banks the financial data normally requested of borrowers with the type and size of loans he had.

As we walked through each individual loan scenario, my goal was to get him thinking differently:

- If this request is something you really want, how can you first help the lender?
- What is the lender feeling or thinking at this point? Will your request compound his problems or provide him with opportunities?
- You are requesting something of the lender; what will you bring to the party? What are you also

doing to positively affect your cash flow – cutting expenses? increasing revenues?
- On your cash flow can you quantify the effects of what you are requesting?
- Can you prove what your cash flow will be like in six months with or without approval of your requests? In other words, do you have cash flow projections?
- In a worst case scenario, what will you do?

My goal was to have Steve do several things, most likely out of his normal style, when approaching a banker:

- Think for the banker. Provide as much information as the banker needs in a format that can easily and readily be used to prepare a loan presentation and submit it to a loan committee or an approving person. Don't make the banker treat you like a hostile witness on the witness stand. Be proactive. Help him help you!
- Improve the relationship with the banker by seeking first to understand his needs and what he is currently going through. Act on the knowledge or information learned by communicating with the banker regarding your loan request.
- Know and understand the laws and policies the bank follows relating to your loans so you won't be surprised. Gear your plans around what you know they are able to do.
- Work with your strengths. Get professional help on those things you will need to provide that are not in your expertise. Remember this is life and death for your business; put your best foot forward, not your least expensive or cheapest.

- Business is relational. Do all you can to develop and sustain this relationship. The banker IS your partner and you DO need his/her partnership!
- Don't give the bank any reason to be critical before you approach them with your request. Make sure there are no outstanding loan exceptions, past dues or overdrafts. Clean the slate.

As I coached Steve on these and other questions and helped him think through and prepare the written requests, I sensed a different attitude. He seemed more confident and optimistic about the prospects for his business in the coming months. I could also feel a sense of peace and resolve return because, through the coaching, he better understood the mindset of the bankers, what they were dealing with and how they would view his request. He now had information in hand that would answer almost all their questions and in a format they could readily use to save them time. He was seeing his bankers as human beings who really would want to help him.

As we were finishing Steve turned to me and said,

"It makes perfect sense to me now, especially your concept of thinking for the banker and providing cash flow projections!"

Several days later Steve called after his first banker's meeting. He was excited. He had received a favorable response. He was thankful I had insisted he "think for his banker" and prepare and provide cash flow projections along with all the other information the banker needed. He related how the president of the bank said to him,

"This schedule is perfect. I can tell exactly what's going on with the cash. It makes perfect sense to me."

The next day he called again ecstatic. He had a second approval! After he had presented the proposed debt restructuring, the loan officer said, "I can see clearly where the cash has gone and where you expect it to go over the next twelve months. Because you have presented me with everything I need in a format I can use and understand, I'm able to give you a quick approval."

Later that afternoon Steve called again, ***"They all gave us the new payment terms we requested and needed"***

As we were saying our goodbyes and planning a date and place for celebrating his success, I heard this noise like a rock hitting metal. "What was that?" I asked. He laughed, "My pill case! I won't need them anymore!"

Romancing the Loan

Introduction

Who is this book written for?

Business owners and entrepreneurs who are:

- actively involved in the pursuit of their dream.
- taking risks daily to bring about success in their business.
- working far too many hours, trying to do too many things themselves because they feel they can do it better themselves.
- aware they don't always have it all together, make mistakes and end up addressing the symptom rather than taking some time and hard work to discover and correct the root cause of a problem.
- wanting and needing to spend the majority of their time in the area of their strengths.
- uninformed about borrowing money and what to do to obtain or renew a loan in the new economic environment.
- unaware of the importance and value of establishing and cultivating a strong relationship with a lender.

The past thirty plus years I have spent serving and working with you, the business owner, because I love working with individuals who lead their own businesses. You are, in my opinion, the backbone of this country. I understand some of the pressures you face. I've witnessed the risks of success and failure and seen the results of the temptations to compromise. I've heard your terrors of worry in the middle of the night over your businesses, your families, your employees and the customers you were losing or missing.

I'm like the doctor who gets emotionally attached to his patients when, throughout his education and training, he is warned not to. "You cannot get too close to your patients," he is told, "or you will lose all objectivity." In the business lending arena one is given similar advice.

But how can you not get close to your clients? You are instructed, coached and paid to go out and get clients and build relationships for life.

How does one do his job without getting involved mentally and emotionally?

I was a business lender in Texas in the mid 80's during the oil and gas and real estate busts and witnessed emotional ups and downs caused not only by the economic cycles. In mid 2008, many in the US found themselves going through similar economic challenges and small businesses were faced with weathering a storm. I felt driven to do something to provide you some help. I decided to do what I know best in a way that will touch as many as possible – write a book about how you, the business owner, with all you have to do and worry about, can best position yourself to obtain the loans you need to fuel your businesses. If applied, my suggestions will help you get back into the game of obtaining loans you need much faster than trying to pick up the often confusing, vague and conflicting signals from the lending industry.

This book is a tool to serve you for a lifetime of growth and success that you seek for your business. Some of you may feel each day, each occurrence, each transaction is a battle to be won. I feel businesses are in a new era and Einstein's words "the significant problems we face cannot be solved at the level of thinking that created them" are still relative today. When just starting my lending career, I heard "New occasions teach new duties" which certainly fits today's business environment. I believe businesses will need to be more relational than ever before in order to be successful and that entails learning new and better ways to relate to people.

Leonard Sweet, in his book, "Summoned to Lead", **http://browseinside.zondervan.com/index.aspx?is bn13=9780310232223**_shares some of the harrowing adventures of explorer Ernest Shackleton's mission in 1914 to cross the Antarctic. Of all the exploration stories, Shackleton's is one of the greatest. He was a man who had a passion for extreme adventure. In 1908 Shackleton was the first explorer to come within 100 miles of the South Pole, but failed in his quest to reach the Pole. The mission actually becomes five historic survival stories with each involving heroism of the highest degree possible and each a success against all odds. The fact that Shackleton never lost one man makes his story truly incredible. "One of the reasons Shackleton failed to reach the Pole is that relationships were more important to him than achievement, colleagues more important than conquests and campaigns."[1] Success of the mission and personal honors were secondary to the value of his relationship to his crew.

> **The purpose of a relationship is to lift each other up. To honor and cherish and revere the other, not hold the other underwater until the person yells, "I give up. You win!"**
> Laurie Beth Jones

2009 and beyond is a new era of exploration for business and every business owner is an explorer sailing into uncharted waters. Until now the primary purpose of an organization has been about making money. While machines have a *sole* purpose, to make money, an organization, comprised of people and dependent on relationships, has a *soul* purpose. The soul purpose should first and foremost be about actualizing a higher intention – to serve the good of all; the money will follow. What will your legacy be? How will relationships you currently have and will develop fit into your legacy?

Business relationships in America tend to focus first on the business and then consider developing a relationship- a money-minded versus relationship-minded philosophy. Success magazine reported in its October 2009 issue that when people were asked to rank in order of importance three areas (relationships and family, personal development and health, career and achievements), relationships and family were No. 1. The same people listed relationships and family last when asked to rank the amount of time and mental energy invested in each of the three categories. There appears to be a huge disconnect

---

[1] Leonard Sweet, *Summoned to Lead, (Grand Rapids, Mich., Zondervan), P. 24.*

between what people believe and what people actually do.

I believe when times get hard economically it is only the web and fiber of your relationships that carry you through. The Bible speaks a great deal about business and economics and underlying every principle Jesus taught is the importance of relationships. Matthew 22:37-40 says, "Love the Lord your God with all your heart, soul and mind...love your neighbor as much as you love yourself." This principle is the sum of all the law and wisdom of God.

This principle is the basics of what I call *relationship economics*. Economics can be defined as the science and study of the flow of capital in production, distribution and consumption of goods and services. My definition of relationship economics is the science (understanding) of human capital along with the flow and application of love between individuals to serve one another in society. Imagine if your business focus first became one of developing relationships, rather than one of money and how wealthy you might become.

When my wife and I got married, she wanted us to write and say our own vows. Doing so would make the ceremony and our life together more meaningful and would give something to guide, live up to and keep us on course. Writing well is a gift for my wife but was a little more difficult for me and I have to admit I felt some pressure. About a week before the wedding, I only had a general idea of what I wanted to say until I heard something on the radio that gave me an idea that would put the vows into one cohesive message. I bought a small silver jewelry box and had it ready to give her during the reciting of my vows. I was excited because I felt my words and act were going to represent my love for my wife and my commitment to our marriage. Here is a portion of what I said:

> "Marriage is like this box I hold in my hand, which is now empty, representing the beginning of our adventure together. I pledge and commit to keep this box filled daily with love, service and praise. I give this box to you today as a memorial of our marriage and my commitment to keep it full."

As long as I extended to her love, respect, compassion, honor and trust, the box would remain closed. She would open it to let me know if I needed to 'fill the box up again'. The emphasis of this gesture was that this was a daily commitment, not something every once in a while or on special holidays. She must have been impressed, because she said "YES!" We not only review our vows to remind ourselves of what we have committed to, but check in with each other as life events bring changes or additions that need to be considered for future harmony.

Like marriage, any healthy business relationship takes work and to make it satisfactory for both parties, there must be openness, communication and commitment.

If you are ready to start receiving a "YES" on your next loan application then read on!

The new combination to the loan vault will be expanded on in the following principles:

1. Date your lender
2. Seek first to understand
3. Connect and remain connected
4. Speak the lender's language
5. Plan first to succeed
6. Take action on the knowledge you learned while dating
7. Reposition yourself in the lender's mind
8. Think for your lender
9. Follow the laws of success
10. Keep selling for success
11. Work with your strengths (not your weaknesses)
12. Be a peacemaker
13. Use 20-20 foresight
14. Relationships are all about LOVE

WARNING!!: Reading and applying the concepts of this book may dramatically change and improve your life if:

1. You need or want to improve your relationship with your lender(s)
2. You want less stress in your life
3. You want to improve the probability of getting a **"YES"** the next time you apply for a loan.

In this book you will find me frequently referring to biblical passages. I do this because I feel people sometimes don't realize or miss all the practical business principles in the Bible. Who better to advise about running a business than the oldest and most successful business owner of all time, God! I believe God wants each one of us to be prosperous and joyful in both our personal and business lives. This is very evident in Jeremiah 29:11, "For I know the plans I have for you," says the Lord. "They are plans for good and not for evil, to give you a future and a hope."

> *In a time of drastic change, it is the learner who inherits the future. The learned (experts) usually find themselves equipped to live in a world that no longer exists*
> Eric Hoffer

Chapter 1

So You Think You Want a Loan?

> *He that would have fruit must climb the tree*
> Thomas Fuller

Have the troubled economy and stricter regulations surrounding business lending been a roadblock for you to obtain loans?

Since mid 2008

a dramatic shift has occurred in the approval process of business lending,

meaning, you cannot approach lenders in the same way you have done in the past. Advice from a professional, who has been a vault keeper, to help you learn the new ways to obtain loans, what information to present and how to present it to lenders, can help you obtain the new combination to the vault!

While I make no guarantees you will receive a "YES" when applying for a loan, applying the concepts in this book will improve understanding and appreciation for you and your business by your lender, leading to an improved relationship and greater success in your business.

Value may or may not be a concept that you readily acknowledge and consciously think about. If you don't create value – no one buys your product or services – you go out of business. If your business brings value to others (defined as something of worth, importance, significance, usefulness, meaning, help or profit), they in turn are willing to exchange something they have of value (usually currency).

Do you agree that bringing value to your customers and all your stakeholders creates a focus for your business that has all sorts of positive repercussions?

Creating value doesn't eliminate profit. It shifts the focus to creating a mutually beneficial relationship between you and your customers which then leads not only to short-term profit, but to potential for long-term benefits for both parties.

Business is primarily about relationships.

Andrew Carnegie started in poverty and built one of the world's greatest business empires in steel. Someone asked him what he believed about the future of his businesses. He said, "You can take from me all my plants. You can take from me all my money. You can take from me all my equipment. But if you leave me my men, I will build it all again."[2] Carnegie's genius was that he knew an organization is not finances or techniques or equipment. It is people.

---

[2] BrainyQuote.com "Andrew Carnegie Quotes," http://www.brainyquote.com/quotes/authors/a/andrewcarnegie.html

In general, to have a stronger, more efficient and productive business, your business relationships must become stronger. Little is accomplished in business without people. People are all created with legitimate emotional needs (significance, authority, honor, peace of mind, security, love and acceptance, the need to be understood) that, if not met, will suffer. Since you spend at least 70% of your waking hours involved with your work or business, would you agree many of your emotional needs should be met in and through your work experiences?

I suggest you approach lenders like they are people with whom you desire a genuine relationship, rather than someone just to meet your wants and needs. Like constructing a bridge between two sides of a river, good relationships can be built.

Eric Beck, founder and CEO of Total Integration LLC **http://www.totalintegrationnow.com/** states, "Intentionality has something to do with good relationships and relationships are comprised of two common denominators – people and trust – both transactions of the heart".[3] Since business is really relational, you have to genuinely care more about the relationship than the result to build success. Beck further states, "You must become a student of the other person, learn their language, show real respect and honor by taking the time to learn about them. Pay attention to them." [4]

---

3   http://ericjeffersonbeck.com/?p=847
4   http://ericjerrersonbeck.com/?p=847

It may be time to build a new relationship with your lender!

If you want the lender to pay more attention to you, your focus must primarily be on the relationship, and secondarily on *your* wants and needs. How do you convey this? It starts with words you use in talking with the lender. Are you talking about them or you? If you want the lender to value you, find out about the lender and show genuine interest in getting to know him/her. This may be hard to do initially. When you first show the lender honor and respect, this can set the tone for receptivity to hear about you, your business and your needs (in that order).

Which of the following is a picture of how you operate your business?

You notice your checking account balance is getting low; you are experiencing difficulties in getting some of your receivables to pay in a timely manner; you have payroll to be paid Friday afternoon and this is Wednesday morning:

- You decide to borrow some money, not only to cover the upcoming payroll, but since your account balance is so low and receivables are slow in paying, why not ask for more than you need. Isn't that what the "experts" always say to do? You go to the bank where you have a depository relationship and request to see a loan officer.

- You decide to borrow some money. You know you need to take something with you to the bank, but don't know what exactly, so you call your

36

bookkeeping service to see if they can give you some advice. They tell you to take tax returns for the last several years. Since you haven't given them anything for the current year (2009), they cannot prepare an interim financial statement for you to take. But that is okay, the bank has all your deposit and check records and isn't that really all they need? Your bookkeeping service also informs you that since you filed an extension for your business, which will not be ready until October 15 and this is August 15, you don't have a 2008 return to give the bank. You get copies of your 2006 and 2007 returns, go to the bank and request to see a loan officer.

- During your weekly meeting with your bookkeeper going over and updating you cash flow projections for the next six months, you notice that the negative trend in your receivables turnover is continuing and even increasing.

You adjust your cash flow projections, allowing for continuation of this trend, to determine what affect it will have on your cash balances over the next six months.

You both notice that two months from now you will begin to run a deficit cash balance if some action isn't taken now. You call in your accounts receivable manager and make plans to take several steps to immediately reduce the trend.

You also decide to call your lender for an appointment to discuss what your possible future cash flow situation looks like, the steps being implemented to correct the situation, discuss where the business currently is financially by bringing him or her the most current interim financial statement and cash flow projections and discuss an increase to your existing line of credit to provide coverage of any shortfalls should they actually occur.

Let's switch roles. I know you wouldn't want to be one, but let's imagine you are now the lender. What scenario would you prefer? Why?

A strong relationship with your lender is a very important ingredient to a well-financed business, which then can better take advantage of market opportunities when they arise. Owners of such businesses are able to sleep easier at night than those who struggle with cash flow issues.

Keeping lenders informed about major business decisions and activities will go a long way in developing trust and cementing a strong relationship. Lenders will provide better financing for relationship-based borrowers who keep them well informed about good as well as bad news in the business. Businesses that have strong financial management and institute good financial procedures and controls will also be looked on favorably by lenders.

The economic, financial and political events of the third and fourth quarters of 2008 led to a huge paradigm shift in most industries, markets and business practices. I don't believe such a shift, or new set of operating rules, has so completely dominated since the events of 9-11 or the skyrocketing inflation, interest rates and gas shortages of the early 70's. Few individuals and businesses are unaffected today.

Changes are continually happening around us requiring new ways of seeing and operating. Change at times can be difficult or uncomfortable. It is said the only person who likes change is a baby with a wet diaper. My experience in the business lending industry was that change was not welcome, by lenders or borrowers.

In late 2008 I read a New York Times article titled 'Worried Banks Sharply Reduce Business Loans', relating the plight of a business owner who received a negative response from the bank upon receiving his loan request. I had a 50-yard-line, front row seat as a business lender for over 30 years and wasn't surprised by the article since banks today are much more cautious with their loans and keep raising the bar for who and what warrants receiving a loan.

The resulting meltdown in the financial markets from problems in the mortgage industry, construction and housing industries, and higher unemployment and layoffs has caused lenders to experience huge delinquencies, foreclosures, repossessions and losses. Consequently, lenders have tightened up on loan and loan renewal requirements, are reevaluating collateral positions, require more equity and in many instances have raised interest rates and fees.

I relate the havoc on businesses of all sizes, in all industries, to that of a major wreck in a NASCAR or Indy 500 car race. After a major wreck, everyone goes back to the starting line. In the wake of this financial wreck almost every company, large or small, is being called back to square one and all must play by the same rules. **'Romancing the Loan'** is written to help business owners with this restart –to get off the starting line fast with their lenders.

"New occasions teach new duties". These times are indeed new and in order to succeed with lenders you might just need to learn or create new ways to get what you want. Like in dating, the 'lines' used years ago will not work today and you can't just rely on your looks and sparkling personality. Lenders will have to be 'romanced'. Borrowers must come up with new lines and evidence that they are worthy of being taken seriously. Every day must be like Valentine's Day in the new paradigm for borrowers.

A man was asked if he regularly told his wife he loves her and he replied, "I told her I loved her the day we were married and I would let her know if that ever changed!" For most men the concept that every day is Valentine's Day (romancing their wives) is enough to make them weak at the knees. In courting your future spouse, you probably did some things you really didn't like or want to do – things out of your comfort zone – but you were focused on the goal. When you proposed, the wedding was just the beginning of building and nurturing a long, satisfying relationship.

What comes to your mind when I mention Valentine's Day? I ask this question often when I speak and it is interesting to hear the responses as well as observe people's faces, especially men's. Usually about 50% of the responses I receive are "romance". I then ask, "What is important to you about romance?" Responses to this question are: (of course the order varies depending on the gender!) sex, respect, sharing quality time, listening with intent, giving and receiving the gift of attention, showing interest, care, consideration, significance, acceptance and understanding.

Romance is or can be the on-ramp to people's hearts. What if you treated your lender(s) like it was Valentine's Day each day and provided your lender with greater understanding, respect, consideration or significance? What do you think would happen with your relationship? The following chapters will help guide you to a better relationship with your lender by showing you how to romance your lender.

Would you like to hear "YES" from your lender?

Brian Tracy's quote below describes what it's like getting a loan today from the business owner's perspective: "Life is like a combination lock. Your job is to find the right numbers so you can have anything you want".

Business owners are looking harder than ever for the 'numbers' to open the combination of the loan vault.

In the case of securing your business financing, the type of knowledge gained and actions recommended in the following chapters help open the combination with your lender to get the funding you require.

During my years in lending I didn't view myself as a traditional lender. In networking when asked what I did during those years, I responded, "I'm in the construction industry." The next question would always be, "What type of construction?" or "What do you build?" When I'd say, "I build bridges", I often would see a questioning look as to where around here the bridges were being built. Holding my hands apart I would respond, "I work with business owners who are attempting to get from here to here," motioning from my left to right hand. "I am employed as a loan officer with a bank and I use loans and my network of contacts to

build bridges for business owners to help them get from where they currently are to where they want to take their business".

My goal with this book is to help you view your lender in a different light and see him or her as your contractor to aid you in the building of your company. As in any construction project, there must first be planning. Plans need to be drawn so the contractor (lender) has something to go by. "Banks will lend you money if you can prove you don't need it." This observation by Mark Twain is becoming more of a reality.

I often look to the Bible to help lead me and show me how to do business, therefore I asked, "What does the Bible say regarding borrowing and how does that help one obtain a loan?" The Bible provides instruction for business owners on how to connect with others and build relationships as well as how and when to borrow money.

The Bible does not prohibit debt but says in Proverbs 22:7, "Just as the rich rule the poor, so the borrower is servant to the lender." God didn't create people to be slaves, yet people continue to borrow more and more money without regard to the consequences, thus putting themselves possibly in slavery to their lenders. Galatians 5:1 says that Jesus came to set us free. There are many types of slavery or bondages you can experience in this world; two are: incorrect thinking and excessive debt. Obtaining God's knowledge and wisdom, or as He says in Romans 12, renewing your mind about business, money, dealing with others, and borrowing, leads to His favor and blessing in your business as well as provides freedom and liberty in your life.

Romancing the Loan

Chapter 2

Dating Your Lender

> *Do you believe in love at first sight, or should I walk by you again?* Unknown

There are not many pre-arranged marriages in the U.S., thank goodness, like in some parts of the world. Marriage can be difficult enough when one knows, become friends with and has fallen in love with the other person. I once had a customer whose marriage was pre-arranged and I asked him how they got along and what it was like not knowing the person prior to the marriage ceremony. He said, "It is our custom and we accept it, but it is difficult adjusting to one another and learning to accept each other's mannerisms and personality without knowing about them ahead of time. It makes for some tense times early in the marriage trying to become friends first and hope love follows."

So, what is it that you want in a romantic relationship that hopefully leads to marriage?

- Love
- Understanding
- Trust
- Acceptance
- Security
- Peace of mind
- Honor
- Respect

This is a pretty good list and most people seem to find or experience at least some or all of these motivational needs with the person they date and subsequently marry.

It's been my observation that you just don't hear the 'L' word in business unless it's in relation to 'logistics, lists, leases, labor, licenses, leverage, legal, or maybe lunch'. (or--it's an office romance!) Just as the 'L' word (Love) may bring anxiety in a relationship, two 'L' words that can bring apprehension to many business owners are 'Loan' and 'Lender'.

Most of the business world seems to operate heavily from the head rather than the heart. Its focus is on strategies, numbers, outmaneuvering, winning; heart-based approaches are considered too soft and out of place in a fierce realm of competition. Based on past experiences, many approach relationships like they are a battlefield where one either wins or loses. If you approach a lending relationship with this mindset you stand to both fail to establish rapport and be unsuccessful in contracting a loan.

We are advised in 1 Corinthians 16:14,

"Whatever you do, do it with Kindness and Love."

Envisioning a world of business that is based on love certainly creates a totally different picture than we see today. We all want to be loved, pursued or romanced. In the business world, this translates to being recognized and valued. We want to be special to those we care about, but we also want to be held in high esteem by those we need and value in the workplace. We want business affiliates, suppliers and co-workers to be as open, receptive and enthusiastic in relating with us as a passionate and growing romance is. The term romance may sound odd for a business term, but I think you'll see as we go along, it's quite fitting.

What does romance mean to you?

Maybe something that has a nice, easy two-way flow to it? Have you ever noticed that when you are in the thrill of a romance, everything else seems to be positive as well? You can actually romance an idea or situation, as well as a person, so it is a state of mind that is open, optimistic, giving and receptive.

What motivates the person you are dating? When dating you want to learn about the other person's values and interests – become friends. The old saying "to have a friend one needs to be a friend," applies in finding a lender, who is one person business owners certainly want as a friend.

If you want the lender to be a financial partner in your business, like your spouse to be a partner in your marriage, you need to know about him or her. This usually sets in motion the **Law of Reciprocity**, or it is sometimes called the law of cause and effect, where the lender, in return, truly wants to know and understand you and your business. Important in this process is your mindset. Regardless of what your past experience has been, **the lender is not your enemy**! Therefore, don't look at the 'dating' process like you would be 'sleeping with the enemy'; go for it with enthusiasm.

I believe that business is all about people, therefore relationships. God has set in all our hearts the desire to be wanted, valued and loved. Degrees of these motivational needs can and should be met in our business relationships.

In the 60's and 70's, there was a TV show, The Dating Game, **http://www.youtube.com/watch?v=OEuIlXVtbys.** The person seeking the date would ask questions especially prepared to reveal the romantic nature of each of three members of the opposite sex hidden from view and, from their answers, choose the one they would like to date. Similarly in 'dating' your lender, come prepared to ask questions which reveal the lender's and lending institution's true nature and philosophies.

Usually we get what we seek, ask for and expect to receive.

Do you know what you want in a lender?

Make a list of the top 10 traits or characteristics you want, need or must have in this relationship. Don't waste time with anyone who doesn't have at least five. You're looking for chemistry and a spark as well as similar vision and philosophies. If a potential marriage partner wanted four children and you didn't want any, would you continue? The same is true of your lending relationship. If you are a contractor and rely on construction loans and working capital loans to be able to complete projects and the lender you are considering doesn't have experience in, or an appetite for, construction loans, it would be a very bad decision to move forward with the relationship.

If all you want is for your lender to **"Show Me the Money"** you may be surprised when his reaction is **"Show Me the Love!"** Like the inexperienced teenager who fantasizes he can just walk up to a girl, charm her, toss her a few lines and then ask her to go to a prom, you may be in for a surprise if you get a resounding "No!" The reason many business relationships fail is because they demand a level of relationship instantly that is only created over time.

A secret that is forgotten in business is how to maintain a long term relationship.

Success in relationships follows a path or process, not a single step. Why not approach business relationships with the same standard you do a romantic or marriage relationship, building a relationship that lasts.

The first element that needs to be established is **Trust**. Regardless of the type of relationship, be it personal or business,

trust entails appealing to the other person's heart rather than their mind.

To accomplish this make the focus on them, not you. To connect with lenders, you have to listen to and **hear** what they are saying, see what is being expressed in their eyes and on their faces, emphasize and gain understanding of what's important to them and how they operate.

Taking the time to learn about them and their needs, wants, issues, etc. makes them feel **Respected**. Continue honoring them until they feel **Secure** (accepting, comfortable, at ease). Defining the risks as you see them from both sides removes ambiguity and identifies the boundaries. Security is not just hard assets put up as collateral, but mitigation of all perceived risks. When you make the lender secure by recognizing his or her natural concerns, you show respect and ultimately enhance his or her sense of **Significance**. By your actions and words you show **Honor** and Respect. By putting yourself out there first you will be taking the initial risk. Be vulnerable and open. When the other party finally feels secure they will take their risk. When this happens, **Trust** will have been established. Then action will lead to results**.**

Honor → Security → Your Risk → Their Risk → Results

The 2003 movie comedy "How to Lose a Guy in 10 Days" **http://www.youtube.com/watch?v=qGMaRb4Z2OI** starring Kate Hudson and Matthew McConaughey, Andie (Kate Hudson), a young journalist writing for a women's magazine, has the idea of writing a piece on the things women do to alienate the men they love, which she'll demonstrate by winning and then driving away a man in 10 days.

Meanwhile, Ben (Matthew McConaughey) is an advertising man who wants to land a prestigious diamond account at his firm. Ben tells his boss that he's the man for the job because he understands the fair sex so well he can make any woman fall for him in less than two weeks. Andie and Ben end up choosing one another for their mutual assignments, with neither knowing about each other's secret agenda. Ben strives to hold on to Andie while she does everything in her power to annoy him and turn him away.

Following are some of the things Andie did to help drive Ben away. Though humorous in the movie, these are actually done in many kinds of relationships. These could be titled:

"How to Lose a Lender in 10 Days"

- Avoid phone calls, e-mails, messages and visits
- Be manipulative, deceiving, cunning and fail to tell the truth
- Make him/her pull words out of your mouth to get you to talk
- Always act like you are busy, are very important and have better things to do.
- Try to nitpick every little detail and fight with him/her over it. Insult him/her.
- Ask tons of annoying questions.
- Be defensive or evasive when (s)he asks you questions.
- Don't show respect. Constantly talk about other guys (lenders).

It is important to know and understand what lenders **look** for and what they **look out** for. As you approach the 'dating' process with your lender, acknowledge and recognize that you may look much different to lenders than you look to yourself, in both positive and negative aspects. In other words, when you and the lender look at your business, you both will see different things. Like in romantic dating, you want the lender to see you at and for your best.

What turns a lender off?

These are not necessarily guarantees of rejection, but are red flags of impending danger to the relationship.

- **Product Orientation -** primarily in love with your product or service. Many business owners are excessively optimistic or infatuated with their product or service rather than the customer or market their company serves.

  Lenders want and need to feel reassured there is a good indication that customers are receptive to what a company sells. A focus that is too heavily weighted towards the product or service, rather than on the wants and needs of potential customers, does not give a lender a warm and fuzzy feeling. "Where's the market?"

  Your job is to prove your sales potential is more important than the attractiveness of the product or service and its technical features. Being able to show and prove that your products pay for themselves within a reasonable period of time is one of the most important aspects of the dating process.

  Tying user benefit (what the company's market really wants) to the market is critical to proving you will be able to repay your debt.

- **Projections which deviate excessively from industry norms** – Each industry has its range of accepted financial results and each company will have set its own trends. Projections in sharp contrast to industry norms and past company history will not make a lender feel secure and a red flag immediately goes up. These types of projections suggest that business owners are being unreasonably optimistic or they haven't done their due diligence.

- **Unrealistic growth projections** – Many business owners are overly optimistic in their expectations for growth. Unless the projections are explained and argued convincingly with evidence supporting them, lenders assume you haven't done your homework or you are being unrealistic. Either case doesn't inspire a lender.

- **Custom or specialized engineering** – Lenders see high costs and low profits, in general, when a company's basic products or services need to be altered or specifically designed for each customer. Lenders reasoning and past experience tells them that custom engineering increases selling costs and reduces the opportunity for achieving economies of scale, with both leading to low or negative net profits. In these situations lenders generally don't see the promised growth in sales and profit growth that business owners proclaim.

What turns lenders on?

These are not necessarily guarantees of approval, but are green flags that lenders like what they see.

You call for an appointment and come in at the scheduled time. You are properly dressed and speak clearly and articulately. They ask questions and you respond with confidence and with documentation they are accustomed to receiving. You listen. You tell them what they want and need to know about your business. You prove you are worthy of receipt of the loan by clearly showing you have the ability to satisfactorily repay it. You have come prepared; you have anticipated questions and needs and have made their job easier

You don't have to have or possess all of the following in order to receive a "YES", but having one or more sure makes a lender want to get to know you better.

- **Evidence of customer acceptance** – sales are what makes a company continue to daily open its doors which in turn leads to loan repayment. Lenders want to see evidence and feel your company is market *and* sales driven rather than product or service driven. Cash follows clarity and being clear about what creates value for your customer is highly important to a lender.

- **Appreciation of lender needs** – lenders always want to see they will be repaid. Dealing with a business owner who is aware, understands and is appreciative of this need up front is critical to the lender's mindset during the dating process. Many business owners actually have the attitude or give the impression they are obtaining equity capital, rather than borrowing money that must be paid back within a reasonable period of time. When signing a promissory note, some business owners think and act like the document is a promise to renew rather than a promise to repay.

- **Evidence of focus** – lenders want to have a sense that you know which one or two things your company does best and that it is concentrating a majority of time and energy on maximizing those strengths. In some instances it is difficult for a lender to determine what it is the company does. Often I've had to ask the owner what was the purpose of the company because his or her time and company funds were being directed elsewhere. At times a business owner will be offering too many products or services, trying to meet everyone's needs or will be building a real estate or personal empire out of the company.

- **Proprietary position** – exclusive rights to a product or service, patents, copyrights, licenses for software, trademarks; well established niches; highly recognized brand; knowledge and application of the company's true asset (defined as an earned position in a relationship whereby the company creates value by totally serving and meeting customer needs rather than its own needs and wants).

Lenders recognize these don't guarantee success, but when used properly can help a company become more successful.

One of the biggest sources of potential problems I experience in the business owner-lender relationship is the negativism by the business owner due to either a past experience with a lender or past experiences they have heard from other business owners. I feel that whenever business owners have negative emotions regarding others, they need to renew their mind with sage advice from the Bible: Philippians 4:8 "Fix your thoughts on what is true and good and right. Think about things that are pure and lovely, and dwell on the fine, good things in others. Think about all you can praise God for and be glad about." and 1 Timothy 2:1 "Pray much for others; plead for God's mercy upon them; give thanks for them." Following God's principles of doing business in both these areas will go a long way to make the business owner-lender relationship a satisfying and fruitful one.

"YES" FACTORS

- **Know what you want**

- **Cultivate a relationship with your lender**

- **Interest the lender by your words and actions**

- **Apply the Law of Reciprocity**

- **Be open, positive and optimistic**

- **Know what the lender *looks* for as well as what he *looks out* for**

Chapter 3

Seek First to Understand

> *People don't understand until they feel understood.*   Dave Anderson

If you are a small or mid-sized business owner, today you have more potential than ever. You are the ones creating jobs, providing services and purchasing equipment and real estate. You are the heart of the U.S. economy and it is in everyone's best interest to help you succeed. Finding cash for growth is the key concern of business owners around the country. Are lenders listening?

As you learned during your dating life, not every person you date will be a good candidate to become your spouse. The dating process is designed to audition different individuals with whom you might potentially develop a relationship. Finding the perfect fit with a lender is a similar process. You want to match your vision, goals, needs and values with that of a lender. Just as no two individual loan officers are alike, no two lending institutions are alike; each has a unique set of values, philosophies and policies. So it benefits every business owner to test drive both the individual loan officer and institution.

A 'one size fits all' approach by a lender, or yourself for that matter, is not the type of fit or philosophy for your company. What the lender offers you needs to match your needs and your circumstances perfectly. Be selective. To properly understand your situation and history a lender should spend time with you, listening carefully to your concerns and show respect for your needs. Mistakes in getting the right fit could cost you much more than just money.

To be successful in today's financial markets, you need to know and understand the lender's culture (laws, politics, beliefs, standards, norms). Every lending institution has a culture that is comprised of the collective thinking of a group of people, laws and policies for that industry and specific policies put in place by the individual institution. To comply with the culture of the lending institution you choose, you may need to change your thinking.

Part of the secret to getting what you want today – the fuel to make your business engine run smoothly – is to change your mindset (thoughts, beliefs, ideals and convictions) about lending institutions. The lender is part of a team, not the only one involved in a decision, so the more you have one on board with you, the better the chance he will go to bat for you with members of the loan committee and final decision makers.

For any culture to exist and succeed there must be laws. These laws produce a lifestyle and that lifestyle produces a culture. In lending, these laws are in place not to restrict the loaning of money, but to protect both lenders and borrowers and ensure that the culture continues. This is very important for the financial safety of the lender as well as the whole business community.

Understanding one another, whether in a business or personal relationship, is critically important to the success of that relationship. In each relationship there is an emotional climate. What if you were able to discover the emotional keys to whatever relationship you wished to form and develop? Unlike in the children's story where the miller's daughter had promised to give up her firstborn child in order for Rumplestiltskin to weave straw into gold, to grant your wish for the gold you simply need to find a lender to give you the combination to the vault.

To select the right lender look at what they say in their advertising. For example, today many lenders, especially banks, want deposits and don't really care if the "L" (loan) word is ever mentioned. Many banks are trying to get you to switch your depository accounts or bring more of your deposits to their institution. You don't lie awake at night worried about where you will deposit your money, do you? Few would consider changing banks because they could save twenty dollars a month on checking account services. You get out of bed each day, not worried about where to deposit your money, but rather where to get your hands on the capital to fuel and grow your business.

As your business grows, you will often be challenged with cash flow; you may want to expand, build a new facility or add on to your present one or open a new location, etc. You need cash and a lender for these purposes. Look for those lenders who are pursuing loan business.

> *Offer value. Cultivate relationships. Do it even when you don't need anything in return.* - Jeffrey Gitomer

In addition to TRUST, as we discussed in Chapter 2, another important criterion in your selection process is determining if you and the loan officer have the same **Values**. A tool I use when working with prospective clients to get a better understanding of their values is a questioning sequence I learned in the book, "Values Based Selling" by Bill Bachrach. The process is simple and is what Bill calls "the values conversation."
http://www.youtube.com/watch?v=kW8frVWiPIO.

Following is a sample conversation that illustrates how Carl, a business owner, finds out what Jerry, a loan officer, values:

Carl – "Jerry, what's important to you, personally, about being senior vice president of commercial lending for First National Bank?"

Jerry – I've been in the commercial lending business for over 20 years with several banks and have gained a lot of experience. I am now in the position to really help business owners with their businesses. With First National Bank, I have the freedom and authority to make loans up to $500,000 and that confidence by the President and the Board allows me to really do some good for local business owners.

Carl: (writing "freedom" on his paper) "I see. What's important about freedom to you?"

Jerry: "Freedom is probably the most important aspect about being in my current position. I have the knowledge and ability to serve and help business owners using my skills and talents with minimal intervention by others. It allows me to be the best I can be to fully serve my clients."

Carl: (writing down "serve") "Hmmm. That's interesting. Serve means different things to different people. What does it mean to you?"

Jerry: "Serving others is at the core of who I am. I feel that if I meet my clients needs by serving them, going all out for them, then I'm providing value and that is really what they are looking for in a financial institution."

Carl: (writing "value") "What is your perspective on value?"

Jerry: "As long as there are people living on this planet there will be things or services they value or want. I believe that this bank and I are worthless if we don't provide value. I must leverage my true asset to provide what people truly need."

Carl: ("true asset" is written) – "Help me better understand what you mean by true asset?"

Jerry: "True asset is that quality or gift, not what I know or a physical asset, I have that when provided or used for others, especially in my work environment, produces or converts into value. It is something that people want and need and thus are willing to make an exchange for, usually cash, or have a desire to do business with me. It is critical that I use my true asset to create value for my clients as frequently as possible. Being able to use my true asset daily gives me a greater sense of making a difference. For example, Carl, my true asset is providing understanding and encouraging and supporting others.

Carl: "Last question," (writing "making a difference" on his paper) what's important about making a difference in the lives of others to you?"

Jerry: "Making a difference that creates a positive change helps fulfill my life's purpose."

Going through this questioning sequence will reveal the other person's true values. It would be easy to stop with the first question or two, but to really get to the core of the person, I've found it important and meaningful to continue drilling down. A more powerful connection is developed and accelerated between you the further you go allowing you to better understand that person and the more he or she sees you really want to know him or her.

Asking one final question using their key words and statements will give the green light to move forward or red light to curtail the relationship.

Carl might finally ask, "Jerry, if, by partnering with me to help meet the funding needs of my business, you will have the freedom to serve by providing me with the value I'm seeking, utilizing your true asset and giving you a sense of accomplishment in making a positive difference in my life and business, would we have a basis for working together?". If the answer is "Yes", then they can move forward with getting better acquainted and the process of putting a loan package together.

I have on occasion decided not to pursue a relationship based on the responses (values of the person) I've received. Besides using the sequence to initially determine if there is synergy between one another based on core values, results of the 'values conversation' is also beneficial during the relationship. I've never known a relationship that didn't go through trials and at times emotions will get heated. Knowing a person's true values has been critical to understanding how and why people react the way they do at times. Based on my past experience (certainly not scientific testing) a person's reactions will remain approximately 90% true to his or her values.

In the 2000 movie comedy, "What Women Want", **http://www.youtube.com/watch?v=99-8-9az2To** Nick (Mel Gibson), is an egotistic, chauvinistic, God's gift to women (he thinks) advertising exec. Hot shot Darcy McGuire (Helen Hunt), gets the promotion he wanted as the new Creative Director – a position Nick was already uncorking the champagne to celebrate landing. Darcy, not only a woman, but reputably a man-eating one, is also a very talented ad expert.

Upon being introduced at a staff meeting as the new Director, Darcy immediately puts her team to work on thinking up new ad campaigns for women's products. Each staff member is given a box filled with women's products and told to come up with an advertising campaign for at least one of the items.

That evening Nick tackles the project by trying most of the items on himself. He has absolutely no clue of what women endure to make themselves beautiful, but quickly finds out when he pokes himself in the eye with the mascara wand, experiences the excruciating pain associated with waxing his legs and learns that putting on panty hose without causing them to run is an art in itself. Immediately prior to being accidently electrocuted by a hair drier falling with him into the bathtub, he'd asked himself, "What is it that women want?"

Nick has his life turned haywire when the accident enables him to hear what women think. At first Nick is pretty surprised and disappointed when he discovers his macho behavior does not contribute to being desirable. All he wants to do is rid himself of this curse until his psychologist shows him that this could be used to his advantage! He soon uses his new 'talent' to help his ad campaign. Nick and Darcy are working on the same ad for women's shoes and he sabotages his new boss by reading her thoughts and selling her ideas as his own.

The majority of the film follows Nick as he learns from his mind-reading skills and grows from being an insensitive schmuck to **developing real friendships with his women co-workers, dispensing helpful advice to them about men.** Nick's life-altering ability also allows him to connect with his daughter, to stop taking women at his office for granted and to discover that monogamy and love are for real.

The bottom line to the 'curse' was that it gave Nick a totally different perspective of not only people he worked with, but important people in his world. He saw himself as they saw him and he made changes in himself to make a difference in others' lives.

Seeing the movie again recently raised the question,

What would happen if business owners could truly know what lenders wanted?

What if business owners were able to hear what lenders think about them in their role as borrowers? I know that borrowers would then make changes to make a significant difference in the relationship with their lenders.

When evaluating lenders, you must know what you're looking for, carefully evaluate your options and seek advice from reliable sources. Here are a few specific ways to find a lender who will provide you with both excellent service and a comprehensive business borrowing package.

- Create a list of at least five to ten things a lender needs to provide you to gain your business. You may not receive all on your list but making the list puts into perspective those things that are important to you. This helps in asking questions and evaluating different lenders you interview.

- Consider what items are **not** important to you and don't let the lender sidetrack you with options that don't serve your needs. For example, the lender may simply use their lending services to push or pull customers into their major asset of excellent financial advisory services.

- Get advice from others you trust. Your friends and associates probably have made similar decisions to the ones you will be making. Seek their advice as to the who, what, where and how of their decisions. Find out the institutions they have been satisfied with as well as names of specific individuals they recommend.

- Conduct a search on the Internet for lending institutions and compare their specific offerings with your criteria and with each other.

- Contact institutions, make an appointment to visit lending personnel and evaluate them based on their answers to your questions and how attentive they are to your needs. Get to know the philosophy and nature of the loan officer **and** the institution and make an informed decision, knowing the borrowing relationship you develop could benefit you for many years.

In a romantic relationship there usually comes a time to 'meet the parents.' This usually signifies there are serious feelings between the parties with the possibility of marriage. When the lender-business relationship reaches this stage, the lender wants a site visit of your business and will be bringing with him several members of his team which might include a credit analyst, the lender's manager or a member of the loan committee. This meeting is usually followed by the submission of your loan request for approval by the loan committee.

Just as in the romantic relationship where parents ask questions of the future son or daughter-in-law as to their character, values, interests and suitability as a partner, parent or provider, lenders will seek information such as:

- How well prepared is the management team to explain the business? Are they able to answer questions quickly and succinctly? Preparedness, in the minds of lenders, relates to how serious or how much value the business puts on a future relationship with the lender.

- How well does the management team work together to market the company and its strengths and value to its customers?

- Is the company market-oriented or technically-oriented without consideration for cash flow?

- How well does the management team present itself in terms of experience to adequately cover all the key functions of the business?

- Is the integrity of the management team demonstrated during the visit?

Lenders will usually have made some assumptions regarding these and other questions prior to the site visit based on previous conversations, information you already provided and their own due diligence. Due diligence by the lender might include credit checks with other lenders, credit bureau reports on the principals, investigative reports on backgrounds of the principles, or lien searches through county and state records. Many times lenders will already know answers to questions that you will be asked. I recommend you do due diligence on yourself, management team and company so if there is negative or derogatory information, correct or incorrect, you will avoid negative surprises and be prepared to confront issues.

At this point, lenders know that they are looking at a possible 'marriage' relationship. Both parties will need to nurture their trust, communicate frequently and keep each other updated on any changing or added business developments.

Another aspect of getting the right fit, from a Biblical perspective, is stated in 2 Corinthians 6:14, "Do not be teamed with those who do not love the Lord..." In a business partnership you want to affiliate with someone who will be honest, pull together smoothly with you and see that the work is accomplished, like a team of horses pulling a wagon.

"YES" FACTORS

- **Get the right fit – one size doesn't fit all**

- **Take the initiative**

- **Have the "values conversation"**

- **Do your homework.**

- **Be prepared to 'meet the parents'.**

Chapter 4

Get Connected and Remain Connected

> *Before you can get what you want, you have to know what you want and make a game plan to get it.*
> Jeffrey Gitomer

Experts estimate that 15% of your financial success comes from your skills and knowledge, while 85% comes from your ability to connect with other people and develop trust and respect in the relationship. Business is relational and is all about connections. By connecting I mean being open, approachable, engaging and interested in the other person – aware and alert. Jeffrey Gitomer said it well (and with delightful humor) in his "Little Black Book of Connections":
http://www.youtube.com/watch?v=Om6Yqgi1Gc4

"Connections are all about your friendliness, your ability to engage and your willingness to give value first."[5]

Success is not the result of making money; it comes from making connections properly. People many times will forget what you say, but they seldom forget how you make them feel.

---

[5] Jeffrey Gitomer, *Little Black Book of Connections,* (Austin, Texas: Bard Press, 2006) p. inside fly leaf.

What is important about relationships? All relationships, or connections with others, revolve around basic needs. Through the recent recession we have all borne witness to the interconnectedness that exists in all areas of business – what affects one affects us all. We typically aren't motivated until one of our needs is challenged or not met. Abraham Maslow proposed a psychological theory on human hierarchy of needs in his 1943 paper, "Theory of Human Motivation". **http://s270.photobucket.com/albums/jj101/atent hehutt/?action=view&current=MaslowsHierachyof Needs.flv**

He broke down human needs from the most basic which included **physiological** needs such as food, water, air, etc.; **safety** needs including security of body, financial security, resources, family prosperity; progressing to **social** needs that encompass friendships, intimacy, etc. Higher on the motivational needs is **esteem** which includes the need to be respected, accepted and valued *by* others, personal sense of contribution, respect and value *of* others, achievement and finally **self actualization** where there is creativity, spontaneity, problem solving, acceptance of facts, lack of prejudice and morality. To meet these needs people need people and the higher a person can function or assist another to function on the level of needs, the more successful the relationship will be for both parties.

There is a discrepancy between the current world's systems of relationship and the biblical pattern of relationship. The world's system is where self is promoted by being assertive in order to get people to meet your needs. In contrast, the biblical approach is to meet the needs of others first. Getting your needs met at the expense of another is the number one destroyer of relationships. Every person craves to be appreciated. Govern yourself accordingly and you will have prevented much relationship trouble. You will find that surface differences fall away when you focus on what the other person needs and help them attain it.

Engaged or newly married couples often say how much alike they are and this is why they were drawn to one another. The same couple several years later will most likely talk about how different they are, confirming the old saying, "If you were both alike, one of you wouldn't be needed." This illustrates how people are drawn to others who can assist them in meeting their needs.

There are four basic relationship styles seen in business: cooperation, retaliation, domination and isolation. Almost all relationships begin in the cooperation style and stay there as long as all needs are being met in the relationship. As needs begin to go unmet, there is a progressive slide down the relationship scale. Since the other three styles' names fully describe themselves, I won't discuss them here. The cooperation relationship style emphasizes serving rather than being served. This style of relationship is typified by Philippians 2:3-4, "Don't be selfish: don't live to make a good impression on others. Be humble, thinking of others as better than yourself."

> *"The first rule of give and take is: Before you can take, you gotta give."* - Jeffrey Gitomer

Business connections certainly include your lender. Seeking first to understand the lender, his world, his industry and how it relates to your business, puts you much closer to having a positive reception and the potential for a beneficial long term relationship. In following him or her into their world, be willing to take the risk of being misinterpreted, misunderstood and vulnerable in order to develop the connections that make a difference for each other. This is what author, Jim Henderson, in "a.k.a. Lost", calls, "non-manipulative intentionality – taking actions that engage others without trying to control them and of goodness and kindness that serve others without trying to steer them."[6]

Chances are you've experienced finding a person you think just might be the ONE!   You realize in order for the relationship to progress there may be some changes you'll both need to make. Some things may need to fall away while some may need to be added so you can both feel comfortable in the relationship. Because you want that future relationship to have the best opportunity for growth and satisfaction, you accept those changes willingly and gracefully.

This is also what the lender is saying. If you want to become and remain connected, changes have to be made. It will take work. You will need to prepare yourself for the realities of the new paradigm in the borrowing and lending environment. Some of that preparation may require developing a new pattern of thinking and will

---

[6] Jim Henderson, *a.k.a "Lost", Discovering Ways to Connect With The People Jesus Misses Most(Colorado Springs, Colorado:*Waterbrook Press) p.104.

usually require you to take some action. Again, "New occasions teach new duties."

You will need to clear your mind of old assumptions and understand:

- Lenders will ask a lot more questions. Don't expect credit without answering them. There will be a greater level of interest in your business and more requests for financial and operational information than in past years.

- Collateral and guaranties are back. Unsecured loans and lines of credit were easier to get when everyone projected the economy to move onward and upward indefinitely. With that assumption no longer valid, and lenders experiencing large losses, lenders will look at collateral as their margin of safety.

- Your lender may not want to continue doing business with you. Rejection in any form and from any source is hard. Don't take it personally. Many decisions are now being made several levels above your local loan officer and these decisions are not all about you. Lenders have many big picture issues to worry about.

Several action steps that you will need to take to get and remain connected are:

- Understand cash inflows and outflows. You must be able to understand and communicate how cash is generated and used in your business. The philosophy "I just sell and leave that stuff to my accountant" will not work going forward. Seek help if you need it.

- Begin preparing cash flow projections. A cash flow projection is the roadmap that shows where the business is going. To carry the road analogy a bit further, it also will show if a business is going to run out of fuel (cash) if it continues on its current path. Seek help if you need it.

- Talk to lenders – old and new. Find out what concerns your current lenders have. Are there concerns about your industry? Are there problems renewing credit in the amounts provided previously? Consider locating other lenders who may not have some of the same issues as the current lender. In any case, plan on this process taking more time than usual...more time to 'sell' your story to the lender, and more time for any deal to be approved. Seek help if you need it.

There are many wisdom principles in the book of Proverbs to help you become more successful in your business. An example of the wisdom there about dealing with people and handling business situations is in Psalm 119:72, "Your laws are more valuable than millions in silver and gold." Are you more like Solomon in 2 Chronicles 1:8, who, when asked by God what he wanted, chose wisdom rather than riches; or like the rich young man described in Matthew 19:16-22, who thought more of his money than obeying God's laws?

You increase your chances for compliance if you offer a reason why you want something done. People need to have reasons to make decisions and justify their actions. Usually the word 'because' is followed by information and has become, for most people, a trigger; it is powerful enough to set in motion a patterned response, in this case a "yes" response, even in the absence of concrete information. This is the same as a handshake. When someone extends their right hand toward you, you do the same without thinking. When you want to connect quickly, offer your contact a "because" and chances are you'll be successful.

For instance: Hopefully before selecting the lending institution and subsequently, the specific loan officer, you did your homework to find out about each. With internet information so abundant, it is easy in many instances to get detailed information that will assist you when you finally come face to face. When you meet instead of simply saying, "I'm pleased to meet you," add "because...

- (A mutual contact) told me he has had such a great relationship with you for over 15 years."

- you were listed as a Christian and I would really like to do business with one."

- (Contact) said you specialize in construction loans which is what I'm interested in."

This shows you have taken the time and interest to find out something about them.

I love book titles and I find them useful in my conversations to make points or illustrations. One of my favorites is "Dig Your Well Before You're Thirsty" by Harvey Mackay. **http://www.harveymackay.com/books/book_dig.cfm** The book is about networking and getting connected and remaining connected, but it also makes the very important point of doing the work now. Get ready. The need will arise. Don't wait until the last minute. Be prepared; preparation is over 50% of the battle. Waiting until the last minute only increases the stress and anxiety levels. Mistakes are made when one waits until the last minute and gets in a hurry.

"YES" FACTORS

- **Business is relational**

- **Financial success is all about connecting (friendliness and giving value first)**

- **There is a new paradigm in the lending/borrowing environment – a new mindset is needed in order to connect with a lender**

Chapter 5

Speak Their Language

> **Communication – the human connection – is the key to personal and career success.** - Paul Meyer

"I just don't know what else to do; it's like we speak different languages". Have you ever reached a point in a relationship where you said something like this? If so, you are not alone. The 'in love' state of dating or early stages of marriage seems to disappear over time.   Dr. Gary Chapman has worked with thousands of married couples helping them connect emotionally with each other after the euphoric 'in love' state evaporated. He says through his practice and research he has observed that individuals speak different love languages which can be boiled down to five basic ones: words of affirmation, quality time, receiving gifts, acts of service and physical touch. Each individual has a primary love language and to effectively connect emotionally with that person, you must learn what that love language is and apply it to develop a deeper connection in your relationship.

In his book, "The Five Love Languages", Dr. Chapman says you grow up learning the language of your parents and siblings and this is your primary or native tongue.

http://www.5lovelanguages.com/. As you developed and branched out into schools, clubs, sports groups and even businesses and industries, you developed or learned secondary languages. Therefore, to communicate properly with and across all the cultural lines and groups, you had to learn those languages. He states, "In the area of love, it is similar. Your emotional love language and the language of your spouse may be as different as Chinese from English."[7]

In your relationship building process it's not what you say, it's what people hear that is critical to your success as a communicator. Kevin Davis, author of "Getting into Your Customer's Head", states the number one frustration of customers dealing with salespeople is difficulty in communicating.
http://www.trainingforum.com/090298kd.html
Since you are selling ideas about you and your company to lenders, this concept should be at the front of your planning and preparation and in ongoing relationships with your lenders.

The words you use, whether you are in someone's presence or not, are extremely important in being able to effectively communicate your message, desires or needs. Words matter! Words are the bridges, doors, windows or portals to reach others. Your daily words will help determine how others see you and affect your success. There is great power in your words and the right words can:

- Breathe life into everyone and everything around you.

---

[7] Gary Chapman, *The Five Love Languages,* (Chicago, Ill.:Northfield Publishing, 1992), p17.

- Influence and enhance the accumulation of your wealth.

- Reveal your heart, character, intelligence and wisdom.

- Feed and sustain those around you.

- Bring health and healing to yourself and others.

- Help you access powerful and important people.

- Energize and motivate your life and others.

- Lay a foundation of understanding and reparation where there is dissention.

- 'Move mountains!'

The words you speak will either put you over in life (help you succeed) or put you under (lead to failure).

I read about an accident where a car had gone out of control and cut down a power pole and line. The power line ended up hanging about three feet off the ground near the wrecked car. Many people had stopped and gotten out of their cars to see the accident and help. Some were standing no more than three feet away from the live wire! As the rescue workers were carrying the injured driver to the ambulance, one of the workers came into contact with the dangling power line and died instantly.

Controlled electricity will give us energy to light and heat our homes, cook our meals and wash our clothes. Electricity is extremely useful when we understand and apply the law by which it is governed. However, if we violate the law it has the ability to destroy and kill. The rescue worker had violated a natural law. He came into contact with a live wire. In life we learn to live and deal correctly and effectively with natural laws and that if we work with a law by obeying and enforcing it, like electricity in this case, it will work for us.

Words are much like electricity and actually more powerful. Words are also governed by law – spiritual law. The Bible says God spoke everything into existence and since we are made and formed in God's image, our words too have power – to create or destroy. Your ability to speak words was meant to promote you in life, to produce the things you need and want. However, speaking words that are contrary to God's will for your life will be just as disastrous as violating the law of electricity.

Words are like seeds; once planted they produce after their kind. Apple seeds produce apples and not oranges. Positive, healthy words will produce something positive and healthy.

Are the words you speak to your lender(s) words of blessing or curses? The Tibetans have a greeting that means "I honor the greatness in you, your courage, honor, love, hope, and dreams". Every person has greatness inside them and deserves honor and respect. Do you see, acknowledge and speak to that greatness in each person with whom you come in contact and especially, in the context of this book, your lender? Do you value him or her with your words and thoughts?

What is the reward in your life when you speak to others' greatness?

I acknowledge this is not always easy, especially in trying business situations. One of the main reasons why people end relationships in business is they get little or no praise, recognition, honor or respect. They move on seeking something from others that possibly you didn't provide.

In the early 1990s a Japanese scientist, Masaru Emoto, following his interest in water and how it can positively affect each person's life, began experimenting with frozen ice crystals and taking photographs of them. Since the human body is comprised of approximately 70% water, in his study he sought ways humans could become healthier using water. He learned that water has the ability to record and hold information. In fact all matter has the ability to store information or has memory (thus all your words are being recorded and stored!). This led Emoto to experiment with exposing water to music and then freezing it. A drop of water exposed to classical music and then frozen produced well-formed crystals, while the water exposed to violent, heavy- metal music, resulted in fragmented and malformed crystals.

Emoto moved on in his experiments to writing words like "thank-you" or "fool" on pieces of paper and wrapped them around the glasses of water with the words facing in. Water exposed to "thank-you" formed beautiful, hexagonal crystals while water exposed to the word "fool" produced crystals that were malformed or fragmented.

The value of Emoto's experiments is that now we are able to physically see the value and power of our words. The vibration of good words produced beautiful crystals, or had a positive effect, while the vibration of negative words had a negative effect or had the power to destroy. In fact Jesus illustrated this point to his disciples (Matthew 21:18-21 and Mark 11:12-14, 20-21) when He was hungry and saw a fig tree and there were no figs on the tree. He spoke negative words to the tree and it withered.

We all have felt the powerful effects of positive and negative words spoken to us. Emoto's pictures very graphically illustrate the power of words and confirm what the Bible says, "With the fruit of a man's mouth his stomach will be satisfied, He will be satisfied with the product of his lips. Death and life are in the power of the tongue, and those who love it will eat its fruit." (Proverbs 18:20-21 NAS).

Emoto says, "If we fill our lives with love and gratitude for all, this consciousness will become a wonderful power that will spread throughout the world. And this is what water crystals are trying to tell us."[8] **http://www.life-enthusiast.com/twilight/research_emoto.htm http://www.youtube.com/watch?v=lkbpXRSIUnE**

I was in a leadership position in a bank in which I, as an Anglo, was in a very small minority with approximately twenty other nationalities and cultures, mostly Asian, represented by the ownership and employees of the bank. About six months into my tenure the chairman of the bank paid me a visit. He told me, "Larry, you need to learn to speak Chinese." With a smile he handed me some books on Chinese culture. I knew what he was saying and deeply appreciated his insights. I didn't need to learn to speak either of the Chinese dialects, but I needed to learn about the Chinese culture so I would be a more effective communicator. He wanted the best for me

---

[8] Masaru Emoto, *The Hidden Messages in Water: (New York, NY: Atria Books, 2001). 146*

and the bank and knew the power to communicate was in the ability to understand, appreciate and respect the other person. This was a valuable lesson in my on-the-job education.

How many times have you felt your lenders were from another planet by the way they talked to you; how they did things or reacted to you and your needs? Did they communicate differently – appreciate, think, feel, react, or respond differently? In my lending career I would often feel as though I was dealing with borrowers from another planet by the way they thought, acted and responded to me.

John Gray, author of "Men Are from Mars, Women Are from Venus", **http://www.askmarsvenus.com/dr-john-gray.php** has made a good career and business out of exposing the differences between men and women and presenting solutions to enhance life with the opposite sex. How he illustrates men and women, I feel offers some very interesting parallels, as well as useful recommendations, for improved relationships between business owners and lenders. Several basic concepts and facts from Gray include:

- Gray adopts the 'Men are from Mars, Women are from Venus' metaphor as the central theme, likening men and women, as beings from different planets, to the classical Roman god, Mars and goddess, Venus as ideal types.

- He says his "Martians" and "Venusians" are only stereotypes and cannot be applied blindly to individuals

- A marital relationship is like a garden.

- In considering the phrase "nothing has meaning in life except that which one gives it.", Gray suggests men and women count (score) the giving and receiving of love differently and perceive different benefits from the same thing, word, expression, act etc. If the balance becomes off and one person feels they have given more than they have received, resentment can develop. For example a man thinks his work has earned twenty points and deserves equivalent recognition while the female has only given him one point and recognizes him accordingly. The key to bring the relationship back into balance is communication.

- Men and women differ in the way they react under stress. Gray believes that many men withdraw or "retreat" into their cave until they find a solution to the problem. He considers this "retreating" as a sort of "time-out" to allow men to distance themselves from the problems so their brains can focus on something else. This, supposedly, allows the man to revisit the problem later with a fresh perspective. This type of reaction, by the man, is hard to understand for the woman because, under stress, her natural reaction is to talk about issues to find a solution. With the man retreating while the woman tries to grow closer, conflict can arise.

There are several interesting parallels between how Gray describes men and women and how business owners and lenders, in general, act and respond to one another. Following are several comparisons between Martians – Venusians, and business owners – lenders to show how best to understand and work with and through possible differences in developing and maintaining a mutually beneficial relationship.

Business owners are like Martians (men). When it comes to borrowing money (sex), they are very sight sensitive and quickly aroused by the thought of borrowing money, ready to sign loan documents without any foreplay and/or romance. They tend to 'retreat to their cave' when there is stress in the relationship and can stay there for long periods of time, ignoring lenders who want to talk and work on a solution. Lenders do not understand this type of reaction and longer time spent in the cave breeds distrust by the lender.

Business owners are the gardeners in the relationship. They must water often and sow continually: seeds of compassion, courtesy, understanding and respect for the relationship to grow properly. Weeds grow more readily where nothing has been planted.

Business owners tend to mistrust lenders who don't bother to understand their motivations and needs. They respond very well to respect and acceptance and like it best when the lender plays in their world (visits and courts them at times).

Lenders are like Venusians (women). When it comes to lending money (sex) they want and need foreplay and romance to warm up to the event. Seldom are they ready to lend with just a moment's notice. They want to communicate about every point to fully understand, feel good and trust business owners.

Business owners are often not aware of how their habits (not responding to phone calls, past due on loan payments without calling, over drafting the checking account on a regular basis, not supplying required paper work on a timely basis) aggravate lenders and affect the relationship negatively. What business owners feel is acceptable behavior might be seen and felt by the lender as something that is wrong, disrespectful or even unforgiveable.

Business owners tend to communicate in the language they are most comfortable speaking. Since you will no doubt interact and do business with individuals whose language is quite different from yours, it will be important to learn and communicate in their language, not yours. My friend and best-selling author of "Rainforest Strategy", Michael Pink, gives some great tips and advice on communicating with both left and right brain thinkers. **http://www.rainforestinstitute.com/ http://www.sellingamongwolves.net/store/index.p hp?act=viewProd&productId=57**

Most creative individuals are right brain thinkers. Left brain thinkers will usually think in a linear and deductive way. Most lenders are left brain dominant thinkers and you must satisfy the analytical side of their brain to effectively communicate. With left brain thinkers, to get your point(s) across, communication should be mostly: logic oriented, information centered, numbers justified, evidence focused and analysis weighted.

When communicating with the lender, it is critical that you also provide as much evidence as possible to support, what many times, is a (right-brained) concept or idea. To help get your message or idea heard and understood, here are several forms of evidence the lender might accept: exhibits such as working models and physical samples, testimonials from peers, publications and articles of support, and demonstrations on how products and services work and case histories.

As you have learned through your sales efforts, people decide with the right brain (heart) and justify with the left brain (logic). My suggestion is to approach the lender with whole brain thinking – applying strategies to both left and right brains. Right brain strategies that appeal to the heart are: show the big picture; use illustrations that translate into their language; tell stories that appeal to their emotions, and practice empathy to open the door to their heart.

> *If you're trying to persuade people to do something, or buy something, it seems to me you should use their language, the language they use every day, the language in which they think.* – David Ogilvy

"YES" FACTORS

- **Discover your lender's love language**

- **Speak, approach, deal with the lender on their level rather than yours**

- **Speak to the lender's heart – use his language**

Chapter 6

Planning to Succeed

> **Planning is bringing the future into the present**
> **so that you can do something about it now**
> Alan Lakein

Where does planning enter into the picture of developing your relationship with a lender and obtaining the loan you want? Let me illustrate with a story about my first whitewater rafting experience. My brother's and my families were vacationing in Western North Carolina where we took our kids whitewater rafting on the Nantahala River.
http://www.noc.com/index.php/whitewater-rafting.html

My brother had negotiated the river a number of times and about four hours into our adventure he steered the raft along the shore to view a safe route through the upcoming steep rapids. I quickly saw the wisdom in my brother's actions as I watched other rafters who didn't bother to stop, smash into the rocks or capsize. It was apparent that most rafts approaching the rough water had failed to plan. We mapped out a strategy to negotiate the river safely.

The execution was much harder than it looked from the shore, but by witnessing the efforts and results of others, we knew what the currents were doing and where to attack the rapids. Because we had planned and executed that plan, we were one of only a few that made it through without hitting the rocks or capsizing.

Planning can take several courses. Passive planning happens, for example, when you allow the raft to travel downstream at the mercy of the current rather than steering and rowing. Passive planning eventually leaves you unprepared to face whitewater rapids or other hazards that come up and puts you in a somewhat helpless position.

Panic planning happens only after the raft is in trouble. At this point, as I witnessed from the shoreline, people in the raft were in reactionary mode, scrambling in an attempt to solve the problem. With panic planning, you are guaranteed some bumps and bruises.

Partial planning can get you so far and then, in river terms, leave you careening over a falls. In partial planning you find yourself possibly prepared for the one big thing that sticks out, but not prepared for all scenarios that could happen.

Full planning, as we did in my story, put us in the position to handle a multitude of scenarios like we witnessed while observing the other rafts going through the rapids.

> ***Good fortune is what happens when opportunity meets with planning -***
> Thomas Edison

In the case of your lender, you want to set yourself up for a **"Yes"**:

- Have a friend or business associate recommend a particular loan officer with whom you should meet.

- Call ahead and, if possible, get the senior loan officer to recommend a commercial lender who works with your type of business and loan needs.

- Call and ask the lender when would be the best time to meet with you. Typically not first thing Monday morning (preparing for the week ahead) or late Friday (tying up loose ends). Keep in mind lenders have past due meetings, loan committee meetings and other regular meetings. Any and all of these can be stressful so, to best position yourself for a focused and receptive audience, try not to meet immediately before or after these. Put yourself in the place of highest potential with the lender by meeting at a time that is best for them.

- Set yourself up for putting your best foot forward by choosing, if possible, the time of day when you are alert and focused. Get plenty of rest the night before, wear appropriate clothing for a business meeting and arrive a little early for your meeting so you have time to relax and compose your thoughts.

- When setting up the first meeting, or subsequent meetings, ask what the lender would like you to bring with you. This might include your business plan, cash flow projections, financial statements (business and personal), valuation of collateral being offered, and promotional materials on your company.

- Role play the meeting in your mind or with others in your office or write it out.   It's highly probable the meeting will not go exactly as you plan, but knowing how you want to present yourself and your business in a positive and confident manner will serve you well in the actual meeting.   If you are meeting in the lender's office, take note of personal items such as pictures, mementos, statues, etc. These are great conversation openers and allow you an opportunity to demonstrate you see him or her as a person.

- Plan to take notes about the meeting. Be sure to get the loan officer's business card, encourage him or her to call if (s)he has further questions and state you look forward to giving a tour of your business if so desired. Within the first 24 hours of your meeting a brief email thanking the loan officer, bulleting the highlights of the meeting and commenting optimistically about the anticipated future business relationship will reinforce the positive memory of your meeting.

- Keep an eye out for any articles or programs that might interest them personally. You could simply attach your business card with a "thought this might interest you", and drop it in the mail. This little gesture will encourage a continued positive regard for you.

Why don't people plan? The experts at planning offer several reasons:

- They don't have the skills or knowledge
- They believe they don't have time
- They don't like the hassle of planning
- They don't plan because the outcome varies greatly

These are quite valid. However, I believe the real reason people fail to plan, is because they fail to take responsibility for what they want.

Planning is essential in developing relationships as well as attempting to secure a loan. Results are not always as planned, but at least you will have a better idea of what you want and won't be going into the relationship or event unprepared. You have desires and dreams, yet they will never be accomplished just by wanting them. First gain as much knowledge as possible about what you are pursuing. The key is to then transform that knowledge into action. Planning bridges the gap between your desires and dreams and their manifestations by calling you to action.

> *Formulate and stamp indelibly on your mind a mental picture of yourself as succeeding. Hold this picture tenaciously. Never permit it to fade. Your mind will seek to develop the picture.* – Norman Vincent Peale

"YES" FACTORS

- **Complete planning is essential for receiving your 'YES'**

- **Planning includes what a lender wants and needs**

- **Strategize and role play the upcoming meeting with your lender**

Chapter 7

Acting on Knowledge is Real Power

> *What we think or what we know or what we believe in is, in the end, of little consequence. The only consequence is what we do*
> John Ruskin

Francis Bacon's quote is frequently heard, "Knowledge is power." Brian Tracy's version takes it a step further: "Today the greatest single source of wealth is between the ears."[9]

For me, *acting* on knowledge is the real power. I found shocking a statistic which states that over 89% of the business books that people purchase or download go completely unread. Of those remaining 11%, only 1% of those who read the book will actually implement any of the ideas they find – even if they are well aware that doing so will cause immediate and drastic improvements in their lives.[10]

In order to turn your dreams and desires into success you must take action. Knowledge of what to do is great,

---

[9] QuoteDB.com"Brian Tracy,"http://www.quotedb.com/quotes/2322.
[10] Simplealogy News.com,
http://usmc359.mail.yahoo.com/mc/welcome?.9x=1&.tm=12501185054&.rand=
f1gi94aq1vc26#-

but there must follow a willingness to take action. Put that knowledge into practice.

> **Goals are dreams we convert to plans and take action to fulfill** – Zig Ziglar

I would define acting on knowledge obtained or gained as innovation - using and applying what you presently have to make a change. I feel too many people short sell themselves in believing they are not innovative. For many, innovation is about making or creating something new. I believe innovating includes taking action; doing something to bring about change in yourself, circumstances or things - taking what is and changing it to make something better.

Typically when one thinks of those who innovate and the products of their innovation, words come to mind like bold, progressive, confident, energetic, faster, bigger, stronger, longer lasting, entrepreneurial, initiative, ingenuity and passion. Historically, an innovator is someone revered in society and in business; someone who is unique and has a special talent, a genius.

> **Remember, a real decision is measured by the fact that you've taken new action. If there's no action, you haven't truly decided.**
> Anthony Robbins

I've innovated my thinking on innovation! Thomas Edison is considered by most as a great innovator. By his own admission he was not a genius. He didn't see himself as creative. Creating, according to Edison, was making something out of nothing and that alone was reserved for God. Edison started with something, and made changes until he got the results he wanted. Everyone has the seeds to be innovative, regardless of what it leads to. The key is to take action; innovate!

Instead of the conventional "ready, aim, fire" approach, Michael Masterson, author of "Ready, Fire, Aim", **http://www.youtube.com/watch?v=RvVSVe57gV0** is of the conviction that getting things done by taking action is more important than planning them perfectly. He debunks the idea that everything needs to be right or perfect before taking action: "People who are obsessed with playing the 'what if' game, are destined never to get out of the starting gate."[11] People who take action are rewarded. People get bogged down and burn up precious energy analyzing, planning and organizing when what they really need to do is simply take action.

Taking action doesn't mean you are willing to put out an inferior loan presentation, but it does mean taking steps with the knowledge you have acquired and moving towards your goal. Jack Canfield relates a story in his book, "The Success Principles," **http://www.youtube.com/watch?v=gOKEYhyUE2k** that demonstrates the power of taking action. In his seminars he will usually hold up a $100 bill and ask, "Who wants this $100 bill?" Hands go up all over the audience with some shouting out various comments about wanting the money. Eventually someone will get up and race onto the stage to claim the $100. Jack will then ask the audience, "What did this person do that no one else in the audience did to get the $100? She got up and took

---

[11] Michael Masterson, *Ready, Fire, Aim,* (Hokoken, NJ, John Wiley & Sons, 2008) p.196.

action."[12] To succeed in your goal to get the loan you want you must take action.

On the reality TV show, The Bachelorette, a bachelor would ask a question of the bachelorette, to learn more about her or just to fill in conversation, and she would reveal some of her likes, dislikes and desires. It was interesting to see if the bachelor would then use that information to garner trust and friendship with the bachelorette and receive a rose at the end of the show. Amazingly, many bachelors just didn't hear her, ignored what she said or were more concerned with their own agendas, seeking to impress rather than understand.

As the show ends you see the bachelor who had been cast off, driving away in the limo complaining, "I just don't know what happened, I was perfect for her. She will be sorry. Those other guys aren't good for her. I did everything I could to win her." It was obvious to me and most viewers what the problem was. The guy didn't listen and then didn't act on what the bachelorette had to say, thus getting rejected! Sadly, this is also the path many business owners take with their lender(s). Don't, like the bachelor, get rejected because you failed to take action on what was communicated.

Becoming informed and educated to the lending world, and more specifically, your lending institution and loan officer, can yield some of the best fruit for you and your business. Seeking and acting upon the information gained from your lender will better help your lender help you,

[12] Jack Canfield, Janet Switzer, *The Success Principles, (New York, NY, HarperCollins Publishers Inc., 2005), p.99.*

keep you in his good graces and enable you and your business to respond much faster.

"Knowledge without action is lifeless," says Michael Pink.[13]

"YES" FACTORS

- **Take action on what you learn while 'dating' your lender**

- **YES, is the reward for taking action**

- **The ball is in your court, take the shot, don't wait on the lender**

---

[13] Michael Pink, *Rainforest Strategy*, (Lake Mary, Florida, Excel Books, 2008) p. 32

Chapter 8

Reposition Yourself

> *Position yourself in the place of highest potential* - Dewitt Jones

While auto sales were down throughout the world, one company was not only holding on to sales levels from previous years, but was actually growing. Hyundai's sales were up 14% in January 2009, while all other manufacturers were down. How was that possible? During the most severe contraction in the auto industry in history, Hyundai was able to increase unit sales and grow market share.

There were 16.56 million vehicles sold in the U.S. in 2006 and that number dropped to 16.15 million in 2007. Sales fell to 13.2 million in 2008, a 22% decrease over that of 2007. This drop in sales prompted the Big Three automakers to approach Congress for a bailout. At the same time, sales for Toyota, Honda and Nissan were also significantly down. January 2009 saw an even larger drop in sales with forecasts for vehicles to be sold in 2009 below the 10 million mark, a 30% drop over that of 2008.

In late 2008, I recall watching and listening to some of the Big Three automaker's meetings before Congress and because of all the attention they were receiving, I paid greater attention to their ads on TV. Their message was nothing but features, similar to what they had been saying for years. My question was, "If times are different, why wouldn't their message be different also?"

Hyundai repositioned the company and redefined their message in the minds of potential buyers while the other car manufacturers continued doing what they had been doing for years. Albert Einstein defined insanity as "doing the same thing over and over again and expecting different results." Both GM and Chrysler filed for bankruptcy protection during mid 2009.

Hyundai realigned their message to the buying public to reflect the current realities of the tight credit markets and less discretionary income for its potential buyers. They introduced a plan, Hyundai Assurance: If you can't afford the payments on your new Hyundai-financed Hyundai within the first year of the loan, just drop off the car and walk away. Your debt is erased with no adverse effects on your credit rating.

So what does this mean to you? You must look through both the lens of the marketplace and the person or business you are currently dealing with or want to deal with. Ask, "How does what you want or need affect them?"

Al Ries' and Jack Trout's premise, in their book "Positioning – The Battle for Your Mind", **http://www.quickmba.com/marketing/ries-trout/positioning** is that the only reality that is correct is the one that your prospects or customers hold in their mind. The authors advise you to concentrate not on the product or what you want, its realities, or whether you are right or wrong, but the other persons' perceptions or what is in **their** mind. You then put yourself in the position to learn principles and concepts that will enhance your ability to communicate more effectively with that person.

If you find you need a repositioning program with your lender, questions to ask yourself to get the mental juices flowing are:

- What position do you currently hold or occupy in the mind of the lender?

- What position do you want to occupy in the mind of the lender?

- Whom or what is occupying their mind instead of you? Find an opening that will gain the attention you need from your lender. For example, the lender says they are not making loans at this time. Discovering why will allow you to offer an alternative to the scenarios that caused previous problems.

- Do you have enough time and/or money? Repositioning often takes both. Many times repositioning is a process and the quick-fix mentality must submit to the long term approach.

The actor, Will Smith, is one of Hollywood's most 'bankable' actors. How has he been able to achieve his great success? According to an article in USA Today dated June 26, 2008, Smith said, "I study patterns. 9 out of the top 10 biggest movies of all times have special effects; 8 out of 10 have creatures in them; 7 out of 10 have a love story. So if you want a hit, you might want to throw those in the mix. I just study patterns and try to stand where lightning strikes." Will makes an effort to put

himself in the best position possible in the mind of the moviegoer.
http://www.usatoday.com/life/movies/news/200 8-06-26-will-smith_N.htm

As a business owner, are you studying the current economic patterns and determining what is in the mind of your lender and what is reality for them today?

DeWitt Jones, a famous freelance photographer for National Geographic, has a saying he uses in almost all of his writings and on his videos, "position yourself in the place of highest potential".
http://www.dewittjones.com/celebrate.htm

As a professional photographer, he brings out or produces what on the surface may be a unique perspective to life, but in reality is what all successful people do in an ever changing world.

He says he is not looking for the good picture, but the next right answer. He goes out with a goal in mind and in order for this to happen he needs the right lens, the right perspective. He is continually asking himself, "Am I looking at this with the correct lens. How or where else or through what other lens can I position myself to solve my problem, for the next right answer?" For any good photographer, or successful business person for that matter, positioning is a key to solve the problem or find the right answer.

What about you? Your lender may or may not be lending money at this time. They may be overwhelmed by all their problems and consider you as a problem. Maybe your business is doing great, but getting the lender to respond is creating a problem for you. As DeWitt Jones says, "If I don't view the challenge from the right perspective, I won't have a chance of finding a creative solution."[14]

Questions you might ask yourself regarding your lender might be:

- Do I have the right lens to properly understand their reality?

- Do I have the right perspective for developing a lasting relationship with this lender?

- Do I have, or am I taking, the proper angle to discuss this issue in my business with the lender so he will understand?

- Is my focus correct to solve this issue? What about the lender's focus?

- Is there more than one right answer or way to solve my need or want?

What does repositioning mean to you? Look through the lens of the lender and investigate, ask, determine and get serious about what is important to him.

This is actually what Hyundai did. They spoke to potential buyers who weren't going to take action with the same old "blah, blah, blah" about features. With their message Hyundai was able to displace GM, Chrysler, Ford, Toyota and Nissan, as well as fear in the minds of would-be buyers. I'm sure you would agree that was quite an accomplishment.

---

[14] DeWittJones.com,"Clear Vision,"
http://www.dewittjones.com/presentations_cv.htm

Have you allowed yourself to understand how these different times affect lenders and more specifically your lender(s) and their perception of your message to them? During this time of credit constriction, the way you are presenting your business and your loan request may not fit into the mindset of the lender.

You may need to *fungigate* your message, your ideas, and your loan package so your lender(s) see or perceive you and your business in a more favorable light. Fungigation, as described by Michael Pink in his book, "Rainforest Strategy", is the process of breaking down products, services, ideas, systems, processes, messages, marketing or anything in your business, to achieve an improved, new or different result.
http://www.youtube.com/watch?v=P_ShG3bOUO4

In your loan package you may need to alter, repackage or deemphasize some things and emphasize others depending on the angle your lender looks at the economy and your business.

"YES" FACTORS

- **Position yourself based on the needs and expectation of your lender (or customer)**

- **Put yourself in the place of highest potential with your lender?**

Chapter 9

Think for Your Lender

> *Give me a lever long enough and a fulcrum on which to place it and I shall move the world*
> Archimedes

Most lenders have a multiplicity of tasks to perform daily including prospecting for new business, underwriting and analyzing new and renewal loan requests, maintaining relationships with existing customers, collecting loans made, trouble shooting and closing loans to mention a few. One of your priorities should be to be prepared to provide your lender with all the required information and answers to questions he or she and the institution (loan committee, senior loan officer or any and all loan approving personnel) might have. This is what I call

'thinking for your lender'

I've been in situations where I was so swamped with business loan applications, I would have loan requests stacked on my desk and piled on the floor. I would get a phone call from an existing customer wanting a $500,000 line of credit and wanting to know if he could receive an answer by Friday, within 48 hours of the request, since he knew the loan committee met on Thursday afternoon; or from a walk-in prospect intending to develop commercial property, wanting to present his request orally and asking if I could let him know what his chances for approval were on the spot.

Rarely did I receive requests in writing with information summarized and presented logically so I could easily use the information presented in my written presentation. In addition, I seldom received information so I could easily understand the purpose and sources of repayment; a cash flow analysis that showed adequate support of the loan; financial statements prepared and presented properly; and collateral outlined with a supportable basis for the borrower's valuation.

Many times I'd point to the piles of paper on my desk and floor and say to the borrower, "See all these other loan applications? I'm like a Baskin and Robbins Ice Cream Parlor and you will have to take a number." Picking up a pad on my desk with about 15 names on it, I would say, "If you have everything I need and in the order I need it so I can quickly and easily analyze your request and put it in our loan committee presentation format, I'll move your request to the head of the list, otherwise it will have to go at the end."

Don't make the lender pull information or documentation out of you as if you were a hostile witness on the witness stand

Be proactive. Make the lender's job easier and you will move your request to the head of the line and make it much easier for them to say "YES". As Zig Ziglar is famous for saying, "You will get what you want out of life if you first help other people get what they want."[15]

---

[15] BrainyQuotes.com, "Zig Ziglar Quotes," http://www.brainyquote.com/quotes/authors/z/zig_ziglar_2.html

So, what's the trick? How does one go about obtaining the loan by thinking for the lender? Or should you give up trying to get loans until the economy heats back up and lenders have gotten rid of most of their bad loans and foreclosed or repossessed assets? I say, "No!" Down economic cycles always come to an end.

Lenders cannot wait until they dispose of all their foreclosed and repossessed assets before they return to lending money again. They must continue to seek and make loans. Credit criteria will be stiffer and the competition between lenders for good loans will increase, but they must lend money. If all that banks did was collect deposits, they would go broke. Sure they can invest the deposits in the stock or bond markets. However, the majority of a bank's revenues are made in lending out the money they have on deposit. Now is the time to put your business in the best position possible to apply for and receive a loan.

What are some of the secrets to getting a loan? Some of the most important are:

- Get to know what lenders want and need to easily and completely process your request. Ask what you can do to make their job easier.

- Have good numbers. A business lender will want to see your financial statements and they must be in good shape to be presented to the lender. They need to be maintained according to *Generally Accepted Accounting Standards* (GAAP). This assures the lender that the numbers can be relied on to fairly reflect the financial condition of the company.

- Have timely financial statements. If a lender knows that a business owner does not have prepared or receive financial statements on a timely basis, he will not have confidence in that business owner. Every business owner should have a complete set of financial statements no later than the 15th of each month.

- Understand your numbers. Lenders want to know that you understand your numbers and that you use them to manage your business. When they question a small to midsized business owner regarding what a number represents, they expect an explanation that makes sense.

- Establish good relationships with lenders. Ask what they consider to be a good relationship and set upon a path to be one, if you are not one already. A solid relationship with a lender will carry weight when a loan package is presented.

- Seeing is believing. Encourage your lender to view or tour your business, even if he/she has been there before. As it relates to your product or service, allow them to engage all their senses (sight, hearing, touch, taste, smell) to keep them interested and enthused about your business. Don't take anything for granted and don't leave anything to chance. Relationships will not remain alive and vibrant without fresh thinking and creativity.

- Keep your lender informed. Relationships cannot exist without good communication.

- Understand and know what the C's of credit mean for your business. Lenders want or need to know the following points about your business on an ongoing basis. Tying these into your communication will help them help you.

Character This is the driver of all decisions. Approximately 50% of a loan decision will be based on the lender's confidence that you are honest and do what you say you will do, regardless of the circumstances. What is your character and integrity like? Do good or bad times determine whether or not you are honest? If you are cheating on your tax returns or showing less inventory value on your balance sheet than what you have in the warehouse, are you aware your lender is already asking the question, "When will he lie to me?" What does the lender know about you? In loan scenarios where credit scoring dominates the approval process, it may be up to you to emphasize the value of this "C".

Capacity What is the ability of your company to repay the loan? What is your company's cash flow picture? Most lenders will tell you that if they could see only one financial document when considering a loan request, they would ask for the company's cash flow projections, because that's where they can see where their loan payments fit into your operation.

Capital How much of your money is at risk? Is the dollar amount on the loan request justified by the supporting information you have provided? Lenders work with both fixed and variable numbers as lending parameters when considering a loan. Variable numbers would include how the amount borrowed compares to the businesses financial strength (equity), sales volume, profitability, cash flow, underlying value of the asset being purchased, and so on.

Collateral Does the collateral offered fit with the lender's definition of marketable collateral? Is there sufficient margin in the collateral to protect both you and the lender, even in a worst case scenario?

Coverage Is the collateral properly covered by insurance? Can you service the debt personally if the business cannot? What happens to the business if you are not capable of running it? Are all risks from the lender's perspective, as well as yours, thought out and mitigated?

Conditions Lenders ask themselves, "Does it work at this time in this industry and in this economy? Are the conditions right?" and then fit that comfort level into their decision.

"YES" FACTORS

- **Think for the lender – be prepared to supply information he needs before he asks for it.**

- **Know your numbers**

- **Understand the "C's" of credit**

- **Treat your lender like a business partner**

- **Down economic cycles always come to an end**

Chapter 10

Laws of Success

> **The best rose bush, after all, is not that which has the fewest thorns but that which bears the finest roses**
> Henry Van Dyke

For society to exist harmoniously we all have to live by laws, rules and policies. We all consciously try to obey the laws and we acknowledge there are repercussions if we do not. Lenders also have rules and laws to which they must adhere and many of these laws are changing. The more you as a borrower are aware of these laws, policies and rules, which you also must follow, the easier your life as a business owner will become.

Playing the game of business daily without awareness of the lending laws, rules and policies as they relate to your business, is like a professional golfer who plays without knowing all the rules. Several times in professional golf tournaments I've seen players think they have won the tournament and then find they were disqualified or penalized for not knowing and abiding by the rules. Similarly for you, without a thorough knowledge of and adherence to the laws, rules and policies of your lender, it can cost your business money and possibly keep you from your goal of obtaining a loan.

The cardinal rule or principle of borrowing from the lender's perspective is having a defined, targeted way of paying back the loan. Lenders don't mind taking a risk, but all want to be repaid what they lend. Without a specific source of repayment, the loan request is considered gambling. Cash flow from operations of the business is the primary source of repayment for most loans. For many borrowers understanding or calculating this concept is like catching the wind. For the success of the business, it must be caught.

The question I feel needs to be answered by each borrower is, "What do you expect your cash balance to be six months from now?" Having the tools in place to provide the answer, primarily cash flow projections, gives you the ability to provide forward-looking visibility for your business. Do you drive your car continually looking through the rear view mirror? Traditional financial statements all provide a backward view. So why not use a tool that gives you the visibility to move your business in a forward direction?

CASH IS KING!! If cash runs out, everything you're working for is lost. I highly recommend you visit **www.neverrunoutofcash.com** for information on how to properly calculate cash flow. Here you can obtain a **free cash flow template** as well as purchase the book, "Never Run Out of CASH", by Philip Campbell.

Some lenders are not aware or experienced enough to ensure a loan is structured so a payback will take place regardless of what happens. Few, if any, lenders will discuss this principle with you, so I want you to have knowledge of it and let it be your guiding light when considering borrowing money. I discuss with borrowers the value of proper equity in an asset purchase, the necessity of appropriate loan-to-value when pledging assets to secure a loan, the importance of a strong, defined, secondary source of repayment and the need for insurance to pay off the loan in case of an untimely death so your business and/or family will make the financial transition easier.

For a high percentage of business owners, this approach is foreign to them. Their mindset is that of high leverage, little or no down payment, control or dominance over the transaction, getting it or having it my way and nothing bad will happen. Borrowing money is not like going to a Burger King and always "having it your way"! In borrowing, as in life, plan for the unexpected.

My goal as a loan officer, in structuring the loan transaction to help meet borrower needs, was to protect the borrower as well as the bank by helping the borrower confront the brutal facts of what can and does happen. I would say, "I want to make sure with this transaction, if the worst happens, you and I will be able to look each other in the eye and have peace between us because the loan was fully paid off."

The trickle down effects on both the economy and businesses of events such as the terrorists attacks of 9/11, the corruption scandals bringing down companies like Enron and WorldCom, the gas price hikes and shortages in the fall of 2008 and the chaos in the financial markets and with financial institutions in 2009, to name a few, widened the doors to new and varied risks that business owners face when planning for their businesses and considering borrowing. The ability to go into a loan transaction with as many of the possible known or perceived risks mitigated is important to the viability of your business and the individuals and families it supports.

The insolvency of some of the largest and oldest financial institutions has been caused by massive leveraging of assets. In simple terms, for every dollar these institutions possessed in hard assets, they borrowed up to, in some cases, 60 times that amount. Once any large or small business becomes that leveraged, trouble is brewing.

Consider this scenario, which happens all too frequently. An individual bought numerous homes to initially generate rental income with plans to sell at a profit once values increased. He purchased one home for $400,000 with a 5% down payment, financing the balance of $380,000, leveraging himself 19 to 1 on this one house. As I've witnessed time and time again, instead of the market going up for the houses, as the investor thought it would, the market went down. The investor lost equity, but that is okay. Or is it?

Since the investor was so leveraged on the financing of the house, he had to receive a certain amount of rental income to at least break even. When the real estate market decreased, the investor's ability to command a sufficient rent price to cover the loan payment, insurance and taxes decreased causing a cash flow deficit. In addition, the investor lost some tenants. Since he had many houses, he had a harder and harder time covering his overall cash flow requirement which eventually led the investor into bankruptcy.

In the Bible, the Prophet Habakkuk predicted what would happen when credit was allowed to go unchecked. He wrote, "Suddenly your debtors will rise up in anger and turn on you and take all you have while you stand trembling and helpless." (Habakkuk 2:7). The more leveraged an individual or business becomes, the greater the risk. Creditors have a way of rising up at the worst possible time for a borrower!

For the past almost four decades we have lived in an era where some 'financial experts and counselors' continually push clients to leverage as much as the lenders will allow them to. Lenders all need loans and continually push the envelope to outdo one another to avoid losing deals. Like the investor mentioned above, loans are made with the attitude that prices and values will continue to go up and all will be fine. Throughout my career I've noted, "Good times cover a lot of sins."

There is nothing wrong with taking risks and business is about risk. Go into the decision-making process by identifying as many of the probable risks as possible and then mitigate those risks before the loan is closed. In my opinion this separates risk taking from gambling.

Some of the largest financial institutions, with some of the 'brightest' minds available, made the same error as our investor mentioned above, but on a much greater scale. Companies like Fannie Mae, Freddy Mac, Lehman Brothers and Bear Sterns, with many more to follow, leveraged investments to the maximum. These companies once were thought invincible, couldn't do any wrong and couldn't fail.

Solomon, thought to be the wisest person ever, said, "Just as the rich rule the poor, so the borrower is servant to the lender." (Proverbs 22:7). King David said, "Evil men borrow and cannot pay it back." (Psalm 37:21). Most borrowers go into debt wanting to repay their loans. When you allow yourself and your businesses to become highly leveraged and negative circumstances happen, there is little margin for error and a situation is created making it almost impossible to repay the debt.

Today it is very difficult to avoid debt. However, the key is to understand, with all the information available, what might happen and structure the debt to be able to either have other sources of repayment (liquidity) or collateralize the debt so the sale of the collateral will pay off the debt. Yes, this might mean putting a good bit more down in cash (35%-45%) and financing less, resulting in a lower rate of return, but the idea is to take a calculated risk and not a gamble.

Another scenario happening with greater frequency that business owners are facing with their lenders today is like the following. Matt owns a construction remodeling business in Georgia. Matt's typical method of operating was to obtain deposits and construction draws from his clients, but he would often require additional money to fund customer work before he received payments. Matt was provided with a $100,000 credit line secured by a lien on some personal real estate to help him offset some of the timing differences he was experiencing in his business. Over the past five years, the most he ever borrowed on the line was $90,000. He was never late with a payment and consistently paid down the line to zero when he received money from the jobs for which the funds were used.

With the current economic downturn, Matt saw a decrease in the volume of his business but was still able to pay all his business bills and draw a sufficient salary to pay all of his personal bills. Then suddenly the bank cut his credit line to $20,000. Immediately he was unable to fund his next job.

Charles owned several profitable automotive repair locations and operated with a line of credit from a local bank of $200,000. He was seeking a renewal of the line of credit and told the following story. Over the years his line balance averaged around $80,000 and spiked to a high of $185,000. The credit line was renewed every year except this year. The bank officer explained the new maximum line amount would be $75,000.

In the above examples Matt was unable to obtain credit he needed and was forced to close his business and find employment with another contractor. Charles was unable to access the credit line he needed and was forced to close one shop, reduce expenses and transfer inventory to the two remaining shops. He was able to keep going, albeit as a smaller business.

Across the country businesses large and small are having their credit facilities cut or even eliminated. We are now witnessing some of these formerly sleeping lenders 'rising up'. As you deal with lenders, you will realize that old borrowing rules are gone and you now must acknowledge the new realities and take action.

Several key principles will help guide you through these uncharted waters.

- Be realistic! Understand that your credit line may get cut, even if you have been a great customer in the past. I have talked with many business owners who were stunned at having their credit facilities suddenly pulled after a 10, 20 or even 30-year relationship. Instead of getting caught unaware, proactively think through and come up with a backup plan.

- Is there another way? Borrowing was documented in the Bible, but borrowing was always viewed as a curse, not a blessing (See Deuteronomy 28:43-48). Using zero credit in today's environment is not very practical for most, but you need to approach all borrowing very carefully by asking this question: "Is there any other possible way to move forward without borrowing?"

- Take action now. Take steps to raise cash and reduce your dependence on borrowing. A former delivery company made deliveries for retail stores. Customers were billed bi-monthly and payment was received an average of 30 days after deliveries were completed. Funds were commonly drawn from a revolving line of credit at a bank. The delivery company offered a cash discount if the deliveries were paid on receipt rather than billed, and a smaller discount if charged to a business credit card. One third of the customers accepted a discount option and although the profit margins slipped a bit, all bank borrowing was eliminated.

- Many business owners borrow when in reality they should reduce their operating costs. One restaurant owner, who was losing $4,000 a month for the past five months, wanted to borrow to fund his loss "for as long as necessary until business turns around." He should reduce his operating costs, not borrow money to cover his loss. Losing ground each month is not a plan - it's a disaster!

- Develop a backup plan when borrowing is required. If your line of credit is unexpectedly cut, what options do you have? Can you cut expenses or inventory, collect receivables faster or develop additional sources of funding? Develop an asset list that can be used to secure asset financing. A contractor, whose credit was canceled by a bank, was able to obtain a loan secured by equipment. Look at using accounts receivables as collateral.

- Lenders are changing the rules with borrowers. You may not like the changes, but it is important to understand what is changing and what is likely to change in the future. Traditional sources of borrowing may be closed or reduced and I would estimate that over half of small businesses with loans will experience an interest rate hike, lower credit limit or canceled credit cards in the upcoming years.

One of God's laws to obey in the area of borrowing money is Proverbs 22:26, "Do not be among those who give pledges, among those who become sureties for debts." (NAS) I believe *surety* is one of the most abused and least understood principles in the Bible. Surety is assuming an obligation to pay indebtedness without a certain or specific way to repay it. Surety also means you are presuming upon the future. (James 4:13-15)

If everything goes as planned, you will be able to repay the debt, but if it doesn't, you may be left with the debt. If you would just keep this law, the most you would lose is the collateral you pledged against the loan. This means you pledge collateral with sufficient equity in it so that in the worst case, the collateral can be sold to pay the debt completely. In practice this rarely happens. Business owners normally do not put down enough, or have a sufficient amount of equity in, collateral being pledged. Also borrowers expect or presume money coming in from sources to repay the loan will continue as it has in the past.

Another mistake business owners make when borrowing is not having a defined, specific, secondary source of repayment with which to pay the debt. In a loan transaction if the primary source of repayment cannot repay the loan in full, then your fallback is the secondary source, not bankruptcy or a default on the loan. It's the belt and suspenders theory: If one breaks, your rear end is still covered!

A good question to ask yourself is: "What assumptions or presumptions am I making about the future?" (good health, business will continue to make good income, the asset borrowed against will go up in value or at least will not decrease, etc.).

Psalm 37:21 says, "Evil men borrow and cannot pay it back." It doesn't matter if the circumstances are beyond your control. You must properly secure any loan taken out and must make sure there are multiple and ample sources of repayment so the loan will be repaid. God's peace, via obedience to His laws, is infinitely more valuable than the world's riches. Proverbs 22:1 says "If you must choose, take a good name rather than great riches; for to be held in loving esteem is better than silver and gold." God looks at your heart and wants to see your absolute commitment to His Word and determination, via your faith, to honor your vow or word to your creditors regardless of the cost.

In my opinion the Bible does not prohibit borrowing. One scripture verse that is often quoted by those who say that borrowing money is prohibited is Romans 13:8, "Pay all your debts except the debt of love for others – never finish paying that!" I have witnessed the mental, physical and emotional effects on those who did not, or were not able to, repay their debt. Often the collection process turns ugly because the borrower may: be in denial of the facts, have his or her pride or feelings hurt or begin to lie and cover up things. Usually in these instances the worst comes out in the person.

On the other hand the lender feels abused and, if negative character issues surface in the borrower, the lender feels compelled to take legal recourse to solve the issues, which heightens the already negative situation. In most cases the borrower exhibits bitterness, resentment, hard feelings, animosity and lack of love towards the lender. The bottom line to this verse in Romans, for me, is that it is almost impossible to love someone to whom you are in bondage or slavery.

"YES" FACTORS

- **Know the rules, policies and laws your lender (and subsequently you) must abide by**

- **Cash is King in business credit**

- **Mitigate risks**

- **Have a backup plan**

- **The rules are changing; plan accordingly**

Chapter 11

Keep Selling (Asking) for Success

> ***Money grows on the tree of persistence***
> Japanese Proverb

In my dating years if I felt something for the person I was dating and felt she was also into me, I didn't just stop using my charm and charisma to romance her, thinking I had her wrapped up. I also didn't keep anything in reserve. No, I kept putting the best I had out there because I don't look like Brad Pitt! In the lender–business owner relationship, you need to put your best out there with the lender at all times. Don't hold back.

How do you keep romance alive with the frantic pace of life, work and families today? Is there a secret to a lasting marriage relationship? I believe both questions, as well as many others in a romantic relationship, can be answered in one word – commitment. I once heard commitment described using a picture of someone traveling down a road and blowing up all bridges or ways of escape behind him so he couldn't go backwards or retreat; he had to continually move forward. This picture of commitment has been very helpful to me in all my relationships. I believe it can also be applied to the relationship between the business owner and lender.

One practical and fun way to keep romance alive in a marriage is having a regular date night. One friend also had an annual 'state of the marriage' weekend where they would discuss all aspects of their marriage, plan for the upcoming year and discuss and outline action steps to accomplish goals.

As a lender, I made it a high priority to visit, either by phone or in person, with each loan customer several times each quarter. At the beginning of each year I would also have a 'state of the relationship' meeting to discuss where the business was going and what it would need in the upcoming year and how I could help, either with loans or with referrals from my network of contacts. This also gave us an opportunity to discuss expectations, hopes, failures and areas of support we both had for the relationship.

At times it is difficult to find or make time to get together with your lender. Maybe your loan is on auto-pilot and you are busy with your business getting new clients, keeping the ones you have and meeting employee needs. Your lender might have 'moved on' since you are paying on time, your business is off the radar because you are doing all things right and you are not needing any new loans. If your lender is not getting with you like I mentioned above, I highly recommend you initiate the date. Trust me; distance does not make the heart grow fonder.

Two criteria for success are persistence and consistency. You must initially 'sell' the lender on your vision and ability to bring it to fruition. Then continue to communicate to make sure you are adhering to the lender's requirements and meeting the time line and goals you have agreed to. Does this take time and work? You bet it does.

Lenders are one of your company's most valuable stakeholders.

It pays great dividends to keep selling them on you and your company's success (getting in front of them, showing them, reminding them, and thinking for them).

All public companies must prepare and publish a quarterly 10-Q to their stockholders and the SEC and a 10-K annually, which is a comprehensive report of their financial performance. I recommend business owners take the initiative to provide their lenders with quarterly, updated explanations of their financials, industry information and conditions and competitive environment, much like the 10-Q. Good will comes from honest, timely communication.

Think of getting a business loan like making a big, important sale. When an opportunity presents itself, don't you work hard to persuade your customer that you are offering a great deal that is good for them? Should your efforts towards applying for a loan be any different?

When you are working at getting a business loan, you are effectively selling your idea of the loan to the loan officer. It is your job to persuade the lender that it is in his or her best interest to lend you the money. Like your customers will ask, "What's in it for me?", when presented with the opportunity to buy your service or product, the lender will do the same. You must be as persuasive with the lender as you are with your customers and do equally as good of a job in the "what's in it for me" test.

Another way to look at the selling process is 'getting your way.' Those are not bad words. Everyone wants it their way. You have been trying to get your way since you were a baby. There is nothing wrong with getting your way as long as it is true, just, honest and good for all concerned. In getting your way with a lender you must be able to convince them; you must influence them; you must be persuasive; you must convey a message and must at times be a storyteller.

I mean story as a metaphor for your business, life, beliefs and attitude. We all tell stories about our lives, relationships and our businesses. Story adds the heart and emotions that mere facts leave out and your listener is more apt to have 'buy in' than if just seeing a spreadsheet. What story are you telling about your business? Does the story you tell match the reality you want for your business? If your business is not heading towards the destiny you want, it's time to get the story right. You tend to live out the story you tell.

You are the author of the business story you tell your lender. Beware of usurping the true author's role to others – the economy, luck, high interest rates, bad weather, poor sales, and indifferent employees. Take ownership of the story you see for the success of your business; tell it convincingly, with conviction, optimism, passion and level-headedness and you will most likely receive 'buy-in' from your lender.

You started your business hoping to focus your energies on what you do best rather than spending a lot of time on accounting and finance. An important aspect of continuing to sell your business to lenders is to have or acquire a high level of financial intelligence (knowing what the financial information means and what to do with it) to show lenders that you know what you are doing and thus are making the best possible decisions for your business.

Furthermore, if all your employees understand some level of financial information and how it is measured, especially based on their position in the company, they will make decisions and take actions based upon this financial understanding to the benefit of the organization.

Financial intelligence includes knowledge and skills in the practical application of accounting and financial principals. It means understanding four key elements:

- Understand the basics of business measurement including the Income Statement, the Balance Sheet and the Cash Flow Statement. It also requires knowing the difference between cash flow and profit and why a balance sheet balances.

- Finance and accounting are both art and science. The two disciplines rely on estimates, assumptions and rules to accomplish the end result. Financial intelligence ensures that one can identify where assumptions have been applied to the numbers and how applying different assumptions can lead to different conclusions.

- Know how to analyze the numbers to gain a deeper understanding of their meaning. Have the ability to calculate profitability, leverage, liquidity and various efficiency rations and key indicators.

- Understand a business's financial results in the context of the big picture – the overall economy, the competitive environment, regulations and changing customer needs.

Success with your lender is based on your ability to validate, sell, persuade, tell a convincing story and ultimately, get your way. These repeated actions create the fulcrum to your long-term success.

"YES" FACTORS

- **For a healthy relationship initiate a 'state of the relationship' check in regularly**

- **Ensure the story you tell matches the reality of your business**

Chapter 12

Work With Your Strengths

> *When you work on the weaknesses of your organization you get by. When you work on the strengths you get great.* - Dave Anderson

When dating, I realized and practiced what I knew, rather than do or be something I wasn't. I surely didn't want to embarrass myself too much or too often! I concentrated on making a good impression using what I was good at. I enjoy being spontaneous, outgoing and trying things, however I knew, for example, I could go dancing every once in a while, but trying to be a ballroom expert, well, that just wasn't going to happen. I was looking for ways to succeed, not fail, in my dating experience.

You must know both your strengths and weaknesses. To maximize your success in business, employ most of your time and energy in the area of your strengths. In working with your financial partner, the lender, demonstrate your strengths and, most importantly, get help with your weaknesses. Most business owners I have worked with willingly acknowledge their weaknesses, but will seldom obtain help from professionals who can offset those weaknesses. For example, if you are weak in accounting, let accounting professionals prepare and issue financial reports to the lender. You come out ahead by being proactive and spending time, energy and, at times, money to put forth your best efforts in obtaining a loan.

Every business owner I encountered was extremely proud of his or her product or service and when questioned about it, responded positively as if he or she was a very proud father or mother. Make sure the quality of information reflecting your business matches or reflects the quality of your product or service.

There is financial intelligence that goes beyond the numbers. This encompasses your ability to assess and apply your company's resources to the best advantage of the business. Those resources include the strengths, talents and skills of you and your employees.

I believe a key understanding and application of working with your strengths includes knowing, understanding and applying the 80/20 Principle. **http://www.entrepreneurs-journey.com/397/80-20-rule-pareto-principle/.** Most people assume that 50% of causes or inputs will account for 50% of results or outputs. There is a natural, almost democratic, expectation that causes and results will be equally balanced.

The 80/20 Principle asserts that 20% of products, customers or employees are responsible for about 80% of profits and that a minority of causes, inputs or effort usually leads to a majority of the results, outputs or rewards. By understanding and correctly applying the 80/20 Principle, your business can be greatly improved.

At the heart of this principle is the process of substitution. For example, there may be great waste in your company. Are the most powerful resources of the company being held back by a majority of much fewer effective resources? What profits could be multiplied if more of the best products/services could be sold, employees hired or customers attracted? The few things that work fantastically well should be identified, cultivated, nurtured and multiplied. Waste should be abandoned or severely cutback.

Application of the 80/20 Principle implies that you do the following:

- Celebrate exceptional productivity, rather than raise average efforts

- Strive for excellence in few things, rather than good performance in many

- Delegate or outsource as much as possible

- Only do the thing you are best at doing

- In every important area of your business, work out where 20% of effort can lead to 80% of returns.

- Target a limited number of very valuable goals where the 80/20 Principle will work for you, rather than pursuing every available opportunity.

> ***Don't let what you cannot do interfere with what you can do.*** - Anthony Robbins

"YES" FACTORS

- **For maximum success, employ your strengths**
- **Apply the 80/20 principle in all aspects of your business**
- **Understand and capitalize on your resources**

`Chapter 13

Be a Peacemaker

> **Blessed are the peacemakers on earth**
> William Shakespeare

I require, enjoy and desire a certain level of peace in my day. However, peace is not always easy to maintain. In my career I have experienced people that seem to go out of their way to create havoc and destruction in the office and in relationships. Things do go wrong and emotions and wills collide, resulting in an atmosphere of disruption.

A lack of peace usually stems from a lack of understanding and when one or more people want their way regardless of the circumstances. I've had borrowers tell me they didn't care what they had to do, they were going to get what they want or they would 'run over me'. Stress and pressure go with almost any job. Peace comes from how one chooses to respond to these things.

In his famous prayer, St. Francis of Assisi asked God to help him

"Seek first to understand, then to be understood."[16]

This is the key to peaceful interpersonal communications.

---

[16] St. Francis of Assisi quote, http://bible.org/seriespage/communication-skills

> ## *We cannot change the direction of the wind...*
> ## *but we can adjust our sails* – Unknown

My father spent his career as a business lender and never wanted his children to walk in his shoes and become a loan officer. His reasoning was, "People, in general, care more about their money than they do about their families. They will do almost anything to get what they want." I was young and, not heeding my father's advice, charged off to pursue my career as a business lender. I soon discovered the truth of my father's words. The job came with a fair amount of pressure and anxiety.

Anxiety has been proven to affect performance. "Of all the human emotions, anxiety is the greatest enemy of achievement."[17] writes Shane Murphy in his book, "Achievement Zone." When the pressure is on, situations get anxious and chaotic and two problems usually result: avoidance and panic. Many people deal with anxiety by avoiding the task or situation. Avoidance is also called procrastination and can become a dangerous, debilitating habit. Panic occurs when the pressure of a situation gets so bad you don't know how to handle the nerves you feel and either freeze up or react without thinking things through.

Loan officers are called to produce for their customers, as well as their manager, which can create stressful, often confrontational situations. In Houston, in the late

---

[17] Shane Murphy, *Achievement Zone,* (New York, NY: G.P. Putnam's Sons) p.138.

90's, a borrower was under a lot of pressure to get a loan approved to meet operating expenses. He wasn't being paid in a timely manner by his customers and my manager didn't feel as comfortable as I did about the borrower and the loan request. This was one of many similar circumstances where I felt torn between the borrower and my employer.

I learned to maintain a sense of peace, rather than take a defensive stance, by following Romans 14:19, "Let us pursue the things which make for peace and the building up of one another." (NAS) I had to be a bridge of understanding between the conflicting sides. True peace in the workplace is a bridge taking all parties safely to where they want to go. To create and maintain peace in your lender-business owner relationship, I suggest you:

- Thoroughly research your options. Ensure that you have done your due diligence and reviewed commercial loan terms from different lenders.

- Get to know the lender you select as a person. Ask questions about what is important to him/her in your potential business relationship. Give the loan officer assurance you want the experience to be satisfying and profitable for both of you.

- Before you apply for a loan, make sure you have some available cash. Business lenders want to see that you are investing your own money to cover a percentage of the project.

- Before taking out a loan, review your balance sheet and analyze your cash flow and liabilities to ensure you will have enough money to run the business while paying off the loan.

- Hire a commercial attorney – one who is very experienced in negotiating the types of loans you are seeking. This is not the time to go with a friend or acquaintance who happens to be an attorney, just to save a few dollars, or to not use one at all.

- Poor preparation of the loan application is a frequent mistake and an irritation to most lenders since the information requested is generally standard throughout the industry and easily obtainable.

- Communicate fully and honestly with your lender at all times.

- Forewarn the lender, at the outset, of any skeletons in your closet. If they turn up in the course of a loan investigation without having previously been mentioned, your application could be in trouble. The lender will automatically ask the question, "What else has this borrower failed to disclose."

- Have a well-structured business plan that includes all of the necessary operating and financial data. Lenders also want to see a time frame in which you anticipate completion of any project for which you intend to use the funds.

- Provide any and all information required by the lender in a timely manner.

- It is important that accounting or tax decisions are communicated to the lender and viewed in reference to their impact on the financials. Make sure your accounting professional knows about your loans and any covenants or requirements by which you must abide.

- Maintain your checking account properly and professionally so no overdrafts occur.

- Make your loan payments on time or call immediately to advise the lender you will be late.

- Let your lender know at the first indication of a problem, not when you are completely out of money.

- Discuss any future loan requests or loan needs with your lender before you need the money. Don't wait until the last minute. In the absence of a natural disaster or an act of God, a request for an emergency loan is a sure sign of poor planning. In the lender's view, a competent business owner would never allow a cash need that should have been anticipated approach the crisis stage.

"YES" FACTORS

- **Create an atmosphere of peace for your lender**

- **What you do and say with your lender creates ripples – positive or negative.**

Chapter 14

20-20 Foresight

> *Our thoughts create our reality; where we put our focus is where we tend to go.* Peter McWilliams

Another important criterion of successful business owners is *focus*. If you wear glasses, you know how fuzzy things can look without them or if you accidently pick up someone else's glasses that have a totally different prescription than yours. Defining what you want is an important initial step in almost any situation. Then keep what you want in sight. Anytime you are diverted by someone or something, stop, refocus and ask yourself, "What do I want?" Focus is the result of maintaining clarity. Clarity comes from having clear vision. Clarity leads to cash. In the context of borrowing money, getting clear on what and how will lead you to the loan you want and need.

I found a very practical formula for helping you maintain vision, thus helping increase your chances of success, in Nicholas Boothman's book, "How to Connect in Business in 90 Seconds or Less". He uses the acronym KFC (easy to remember- like the fast food restaurant):
K- Know what you want.
F- Find out what you are getting.
C- Change what you do until you get what you want.
http://www.youtube.com/watch?v=bUQ1WkjsxSY

The key to the loan request process is to make those necessary and vital changes in yourself, in the information you provide and in improving the connection with your lender to achieve your goal---a "YES" on your loan request.

A second formula to help guide you is from Jack Canfield, author of "The Success Principles": E + R = O. "Events" plus "Response" equals "Outcome".   Every *outcome* in life is the result of how you have *responded* to previous *events*. If you keep doing what you've always done, you'll keep getting what you've always gotten. If you aren't satisfied with the outcomes, maintain your focus, be persistent and keep changing your response until you get what you want.

An old Chinese proverb says, "Unless you change direction, you are likely to arrive at where you are headed." Do you have a vision? Do you know where you want to end up?

In our humanness we take our eyes off our relationships from time to time. Fortunately, we have holidays, birthdays, anniversaries and other special days to bring back our focus and attention to those people we love and who are meaningful in our lives.

In business we have our employees, customers, suppliers, etc. to focus on. What is it you must do or what are the patterns you set up to insure you maintain focus on those important business relationships? Taking the time to develop a detailed vision statement for both yourself and then for your business can provide a wonderful 'GPS' system (Guiding Principles for Success) for you and your employees to refer to on a regular basis.

This focal point unites everyone and clarifies what, where, when and how to respond so cash will follow.

I begin my day either reading or recalling my vision statement, which gives me the spark to get me going and serves as an energy boost during the day. Knowing that business is primarily about people, I want to speak or act in a way that will meet a motivational need they might have such as love and acceptance, honor, significance, contentment, peace of mind, security, preference, to be understood or authority.

Vision acts like the spark plug in a car. A car is a very useful tool and has the capacity for doing great things to help in your daily affairs, but without the spark plug the car is only a piece of metal, not capable of performing in the way in which it was designed.

Revealing your vision to your lender allows him/her to go beyond the business information you've provided to the passion and purpose you have for the business. (S)He then becomes a collaborator or stakeholder in your achieving your dreams.

Rather than traveling a business path reacting to whatever business wind blows and then having 20-20 hindsight where you might say, "If I only had....", your vision will provide the 20-20 foresight to directly lead you and your business to the kind of success you have dreamed of.

"YES" FACTORS

- **Be prepared to change your response until you get the outcome you want.**

- **Clarity leads to cash**

- **Use the KFC and ERO formulas in your strategies**

Chapter 15

What Now?

> *"The catalyst for turning around my business career
> was when I stopped looking out the window for answers
> and started looking in the mirror. I realized that it was
> my inside decisions and not outside conditions that
> determined my success. I started focusing ferociously
> on what I could control."* Dave Anderson

What's the secret to getting the loan you need?

In an article published by the New York Times, Doug Tatum, president of Tatum LLC, suggested that business owners stop trying to get loans for their businesses because it had gotten so difficult and financial institutions were unwilling to take on risks at certain levels and could not make money by making loans at other levels.

Despite billions of dollars of bailout and stimulus money, the credit squeeze that kicked off our current economic crisis shows few signs of abating soon. For the most part, lenders still aren't lending money and businesses are still struggling to find ways to finance their operations.

Lenders are very cautious about what they have on their balance sheets. Most still don't know what their loan portfolios are worth; many do not want to increase their risks. That means they're waiting for the next shoe to drop, which most likely will be the commercial markets. Many lenders have the regulators telling them when and where they can lend money. So while you might see and hear politicians on the news saying, 'Lend, lend, lend,' the regulators are holding the lending institutions back.

So, what is the secret? How can you secure the loan you need in such a tight credit market?

> ***Successful people are successful because they form the habits of doing those things that failures don't like to do.*** Albert Gray

Several of the most important ways are:

- **Submit a written loan proposal.** Look at this opportunity like you would vows to a potential spouse; put it in writing. Leave nothing to the imagination (think for your lender). *Spill your guts (heart)*. Where possible document the following:

  - Precisely how much? Do your homework.

  - Specific purpose.

  - How long. Remember you will be signing a promise to repay not renew!

  - What if something goes wrong? What then?

  - Company history. Bring the loan officer up to date if this is not a new lender.

  - Market situation/status.

  - Product or service information. Include marketing/sales plans.

  - Financial history, projections. Document repayment ability.

  - Collateral. Remember the lender is very risk adverse now.

- **Have accurate, properly prepared financials.** A business lender will want to see your financial statements early in the discussion and, to make a good impression, they must be in good shape. A few numbers on a piece of paper to hand to a lender isn't enough! They need to be maintained according to *Generally Accepted Accounting Standards* (GAAP). This assures the lender that the numbers can be relied on to fairly reflect the financial condition of the company.

- **Have timely financial statements**. In general, if a lender knows that financials are prepared on a regular basis (at least quarterly), he will have greater confidence in that business owner. For many business owners the tax return is their only financial statement and many file their return at the October deadline.

  For example, you are in need of a loan and it is August of 2009. In this scenario your latest statement would be as of December 31, 2007, making that statement 20 months old. This wouldn't impress me much if I was your lender. Sadly this happens way too often. Business owners ought to have a complete set of financial statements no later than 15 days after each quarter end. Not having timely financials is like your child not receiving a grade report in elementary school. You want and need to know what type of progress they are making so adjustments can quickly and easily be made.

- **Understand your numbers**. Lenders want to know that you understand your numbers and that you use them to manage your company. When a lender questions you regarding what a number represents, they expect an explanation that makes sense. Lenders lend money based on your ability to repay. Being able to explain and prove this ability is critical for their confidence in you.

- **Invest in your "relational" capital**. Lenders are looking for good clients, to create relationships that are profitable and beneficial to both parties. Find out what being a good relationship means to the lender. Take the time to invest wisely in developing both yourself and business to become the best possible client you can be. Make yourself attractive. A good relationship with a lender will carry weight when a loan package is presented.

- **Investigate possible lenders**. If your lender is a bank or you are 'dating' banks, you can go to **www.fdic.gov** and research or investigate the financial standing or status of the bank. In addition, go to **www.Bankrate.com** and check out your possible bank lenders here as well. Many lenders have their lending hands tied by regulators and you will not know this from any published information. A thorough review of the call reports to notice trends (what they call the bank's quarterly financials) will reveal a wealth of information regarding the bank. This tied with what loan officers are saying at that bank will give you a very good idea whether or not they are able to lend money.

What do you do if you are rejected? For me the thought of rejection was enough at times to stop me from asking or seeking a date. I didn't have any sisters growing up and was never around girls much to really feel comfortable around them. I preferred knowing the girl I was asking out at least liked me enough to say "yes", if the situation was right. If I was rejected, it was always important for me to know or find out the reason for the rejection.

Being rejected by a lender is no fun since egos get bruised. As I've told business owners, "Plan A seldom works. You must be flexible and go into the loan request with several options or plans." Learn from any rejection you might receive. Don't withdraw and vow to never request a loan again. Ask the lender questions. Find out what might work. You cannot experience improvement without willingness to improve and act on the knowledge received. Maybe it is the current timing of your request with the conditions in the marketplace; maybe the lender has little or no appetite for your business or the collateral being offered, or simply doesn't want to do the deal.

There is no law that says a federally insured lending institution must make you a loan. Surprisingly, I've had business owners actually say I was obligated to make them a loan since I worked for a federally insured institution.

In 1998 Shania Twain, pop and country and western artist, released the song, "That Don't Impress Me Much." **http://www.youtube.com/watch?v=XqYp1jpzKCk** In the song Shania sang about several types of guys she knew: a rocket scientist, a guy who carried a mirror and comb in his pocket, a guy who looked like Brad Pitt, and a guy who owned his own car. She thought each of the guys was alright but none of them impressed her and she sent each on his way. None of the guys bothered to find out what she really wanted and needed. Don't give the loan officer the opportunity to say to you the words that Shania Twain sang, "That Don't Impress Me Much."

There's an old story about a traveling preacher who had a habit of priming the empty collection plate with a new one dollar bill before going up to the pulpit to preach. As a visiting or traveling preacher, he lived from the money placed in the collection plate by those attending the service and by priming the plate or planting seed, he hoped his harvest would be larger. At the end of his sermon he found the usher waiting for him with the collection plate with only the one new dollar bill he had put in. "Well, Reverend," said the usher as he stuck the collection towards him, "if you'd put more into it, you'd have gotten more out of it."

As you apply more of the keys discussed in this book, you will get more of what you desire and these keys will help you develop, maintain and grow a strong and mutually productive relationship with your lender.

Times are challenging for sure, but it's critical that you work closely with your lenders to construct a loan structure that makes sense for both parties. Seeking outside expertise in understanding how lenders work is a great way for the busy business owners to obtain a financing package that works well for the business and the lender.

Bottom line – the more you see the loan application from the lender's perspective, the easier you make it for the lender to say "YES".

How will lenders assess your loan application?

Lenders make money by making loans and charging rent or interest on the money they loan out. As the credit crisis is showing, lenders are experiencing problems in receiving back the money they have loaned out and thus repayment is their first concern. The following are all areas of concern for lenders:

- **Risk**. At this time lenders don't want to take on any unnecessary risks so the first issue is the amount of risk they will assume by taking on your request. They are going to be pretty risk-averse so you will need to present a request as if you were looking through their eyes.

- **Character**. The lender knows that the success of your business depends on you as the owner so he will look very carefully at how good a risk you are:
  - What is your credit history? Do you have a record of making payments on time?
  - How committed are you to the business?
  - Do they believe that you are honest and have high integrity?
  - What are your personal assets? Have you been and are you a saver or a spender?

- **Ability**
  - Do you have the capacity to do what you say you will do?

- ♥ What has been your track record in the past?

- ♥ Are you giving or presenting to the lender the impression you are in control of your business?

- ♥ Do your numbers show you have the capacity to repay the loan?

- ♥ How strong is your management team or does the business rely solely on you?

- ♥ Is there a succession plan if anything happened to you?

- **Purpose**

  - ♥ Why do you want the loan?

  - ♥ Can you prove the reason is true? Lenders have caught people saying one thing and doing another.

  - ♥ Is the reason sensible for the business?

  - ♥ How much do the cash forecasts indicate that you need?

  - ♥ Are your cash forecasts realistic?

- **Repayment**.

  - ♥ Is the repayment plan suggested acceptable?

  - ♥ Have you repaid similar loans in the past?

  - ♥ If the business can't pay back the loan, can you?

- **Collateral**.

  - ♥ Does the collateral offered fit with the bank's criteria?

  - ♥ Does the security available comfortably cover the amount of the loan?

  - ♥ What extra could be offered as collateral?

Another important aspect that Leonard Sweet brings out in "Summoned to Lead", previously mentioned in the Introduction, relates to a particular incident of Sir Earnest Shackleton and his crew who were faced with a real dilemma. **http://www.dailymotion.com/video/x6ftnk_summoned-to-lead** Shackleton and his crew were attempting to make it to the South Pole and became stuck (the ship froze in the ice and was being squeezed to pieces) 600 miles from their destination. Winter had set in and they needed help. Where they were stuck wasn't along a shipping route so no ships would be coming by. He decided to take one of the life boats and five members of his 28-person crew and head to an island 800 miles away where a settlement was located. After a 17-day trip, they reached the island, but on the opposite side of where the settlement was located to avoid being washed away from the island by heavy winds.

They were next faced with crossing several mountain ranges that had never been crossed, in the dead of winter and without sleeping provisions. They came across three different mountain ranges, which were dead-ends, forcing them to find other routes and to travel in the dark. As they reached the summit of the fourth, they looked into the darkness below not knowing if the steep mountainside ended in a precipice or sloped all the way to the bottom. They had traveled for 24 hours and didn't have the strength or provisions to look for another route. It was dark and freezing cold and stopping would mean sure death. What to do? What if they hit a rock? What if the slope didn't level off? These were all appropriate questions, however, Shackleton asked the right question, "Can we stay where we are?"[18]

> *Everything can be taken from a man or a woman but one thing: the last of human freedoms is to choose one's attitude in any given set of circumstances, to choose one's own way.* - Viktor Frankl

Is your business in a crisis? Are you in survival mode? Can you afford to keep doing what you have been doing in your relationship with your lender(s)? Doing what you have been doing will get you, at a minimum, no better than what you already have. Can you afford today to stay where you are?

> *The future is not a result of choices among alternative paths offered by the present, but a place that is created – created first in the mind and will, created next in activity. The future is not some place we are going to, but one we are creating. The paths are not to be found, but made, and the activity of making them, changes both the maker and the destination.* John Schaar

"YES" FACTORS

- **Spill your guts (heart)**
- **Prevent lender saying after reviewing your request, "That don't' impress me much!"**
- **Invest in relational capital**
- **Explore lending options**

---

[18] Leonard Sweet, *Summoned to Lead,* (Grand Rapids, Michigan, Zondervan, 2004), p.96.

Chapter 16

What's Love Got to Do With It?

Since moving to western North Carolina from Houston three years ago, I have really noticed and become more aware of color. My wife and I go hiking often and we get to experience and enjoy four seasons of the year and all the vast colors that each season brings, especially the brightly, colored leaves of autumn along with a wide variety of animals, birds, plants and flowers. My life is literally filled with color. In retrospect I realize color was all around me while I lived in Houston, but I failed to see it!

This fall I asked God why color was so important to Him and why He filled our lives daily with so much color. God's answer was that color reflected His nature, His beauty. Beauty is part of His essence. I recalled Genesis 1:27 where it says man is made in God's image and likeness. Wow, this means part of my essence is beauty and color like God's. I asked God again why color was so important to Him. His answer was that the color I saw and greatly enjoyed daily was how He saw me. I was beautiful in His eyes and I was something special as a human being, created by Him as something of great value and worth and something to behold, to marvel at.

I heard Him speak to my heart, "Larry, see the color all around you that you are enjoying and that you are moved emotionally by? That is how I see everyone I've created and that is how I want you to see everyone you come in contact with. I want you to see them through my eyes of love. I want you to tell others what I've told you about color and how I see all my creation. When I speak, my dialect is 'LOVE'. Everyone, regardless of their language, is able to understand love. Since I made you in my image and likeness, when you speak I want your dialect to be like mine, 'LOVE.' Go and speak to them in this dialect. Romance me! Romance all others you see and come in contact with."

God then reminded me of Matthew 22:37-40, "Love the Lord your God with all your heart, soul and mind. This is the first and greatest commandment. The second most important is similar: Love your neighbor as much as you love yourself. All the other commandments and all the demands of the prophets stem from these two laws and are fulfilled if you obey them. Keep only these and you will find that you are obeying all the others".

1 Corinthians 13, called the love chapter in the Bible, describes love as: never giving up, caring more for others than for self, doesn't want what it doesn't have, doesn't strut, doesn't have a swelled head, isn't always "me first", doesn't fly off the handle, doesn't keep score of the sins of others, doesn't revel when others grovel, takes pleasure in the flowering of truth, puts up with anything, trusts God always, always looks for the best, never looks back, but keeps going to the end (The Message Bible).

Those filled with this kind of love will be a powerful force in whatever environment they find themselves and have the potential to create great things in the workplace.

Since I was asking and God was answering, I asked Him, "From Your perspective what does love have to do with business, especially during this recession?"

God instructed me to view others as He saw me and to romance Him as well as others. He reminded me what I had witnessed and learned from Michael Pink during my trip with him and 38 other business people, in February 2009, to the Panamanian rainforest. God's business, Nature, and specifically, the tropical rainforest, is very abundant and prosperous, due partly to the relationships developed therein, despite the poor soil (low capital) and going through a dry season annually (recession). In their book "What We Learned in the Rainforest", authors, Tachi Kiuchi and Bill Shireman, said, "We discovered the most valuable resources of the rainforest were not the trees or other physical resources, but the *relationships.*"[19] **http://www.youtube.com/watch?v=hUklO5oaD2Y http://www.newhorizons.org/future/kiuchi.htm**

Since God provided His business, Nature, for our use and instruction, I felt God was telling me to pay more attention to relationships and to tell others the same.

Since my life's work had been in providing financing for business owners, I asked God to show me how business owners could obtain capital for their businesses during and after this recession. His answer was, "Wealth, like in my business, is in relationships. See people through my eyes of love; romance those relationships. Business owners are failing due to a lack of knowledge and obedience to my laws." He said for me to tell business owners at this time, "If you want or need working capital, cash flow, wealth or funds to survive,

---

[19] Tachi Kiuchi and Bill Shireman, *What We Learned in the Rainforest: Business Lessons from Nature,* (San Francisco, California: Berrett-Koehler Publishers, 2002) p. 9.

look to your relationships and love them according to Matthew 22." He further said for me to "tell them to romance their relationships, especially their employees."

John Wooden, the famous UCLA basketball coach, mentions in his book, "Wooden On Leadership", reading a statement from a famous coach during the early portion of his career that really helped and guided him in his future relationships, especially with his players. He adopted the saying as a philosophy and told each of his players at the beginning of each season, "I will not like you all the same but I will love you all the same."[20] This philosophy is one of the major reasons for his successful career as a basketball coach and provides a lesson that can applied in business and life.

There is a silent thief running free and loose in many businesses today. He doesn't make much noise – but sure steals a lot from you.   All that is needed to help perpetuate this silent thief is to do nothing. Who is this silent thief? Neglect!

Neglect of important relationships in your business – employees and customers primarily. A word of warning and advice today against this silent thief is found in Proverbs 27:23-24, "Know your sheep by name; carefully attend to your flocks; don't take them for granted; possessions don't last forever". God is saying to take care of what is truly important. You might not consider people and relationships that important, but He sure does. What you don't take care of, you may very well lose. Your business may be like a spinning gerbil wheel, but the thief

---

[20] John Wooden and Steve Jamison, *"Wooden on Leadership"*, (New York, NY: McGraw-Hill Companies, 2005) p.80.

doesn't care. The longer you neglect relationships, the harder it's going to be to fix.

Earlier in this chapter I mentioned God brought to my mind Matthew 22:37-40, reminding me of how I was to love all. The next question I had was, "Who is my neighbor?" God prompted me with the Bible story in Luke 10:30-37 that answers the question and challenges us with the way people are to be treated or served. Many are familiar with the story called the Good Samaritan.

The story takes place in Israel with a Jewish man traveling by himself on a road frequently occupied by robbers, thus being unsafe for those traveling alone. The traveler was robbed, beaten, stripped of all his clothes and left for dead along the side of the road. Three individuals passed by the traveler. One was a priest who one would have certainly thought would have stopped but didn't. A second was a Jew, a native countryman. He didn't stop either.

A third passerby was a Samaritan who was hated by the Jews and one would think that he would be the least likely to stop and lend the traveler in distress a hand, but he did stop because he felt compassion and empathy for him. The Samaritan administered first aid to the ailing traveler, put him on his donkey, took him to an inn, saw that he was made comfortable and left money with the inn keeper for the traveler's care and stay at the inn. The Samaritan did something so totally out of character by a hated foreigner and with no hope of payback.

This story probably raises several questions for you, especially as it relates to people you see in your daily business context. Who is my neighbor, and do I need to help him? The most practical and logical answers to these questions today are that anyone who crosses your path and anyone who needs help that you can afford to provide is your neighbor.

Many you come in contact with today are like the traveler: they are stripped of self-confidence, self-worth, hope, faith, meaning and opportunity; beaten by competition, by fellow employees and supervisors, by failure and pressure and stress to perform; and are abandoned, lonely and filled with fear and doubt. Today many in the workplace walk blindly unaware past others (employees, customers, competitors) failing to lend a hand or to serve. Many are too busy, preoccupied with their own lives and are also filled with fear and doubt and fighting to keep or justify their own jobs.

I believe God is saying to us all it is time to take the mindset of and act like 'The Good Samaritan'. It's time to stop making excuses of 'I am too busy' or 'that is not my problem' or let your nearsightedness (consumed with me and my own world) get in your way. Stopping to serve is highly compatible with God's design for this earth; relationships are extremely important. As God has demonstrated via His business, Nature, business and life are relational for us too.

What really makes the economy and world function is people and love. If business is relational, and it truly is since everything starts and ends with someone in a business transaction (an exchange), what are you doing to enhance, develop or romance those relationships? I see or view profits or money as the fruit of working with and developing relationships. Today many in business have the exact opposite view. They work to achieve profits at all costs. Many are forsaking relationships.

I believe God wants people to get it right, His way. Relationships and love come first. For many in business, money is leveraged in order to achieve growth and profits. God's way of doing business is to leverage relationships in order to grow and produce profits.

Economics is often defined as the science and study of the production, distribution and consumption of goods and services. In reality it is the flow of money, or the cycle of money through a business. At this time rather than concentrating on the economy and all the negative effects and on money and sales, I would suggest focusing on **relationship economics**. I define it as the flow of love throughout your business as it relates to all your stakeholders.

My hope is for you and all your team members to make an emotional investment by romancing each and every employee, customer, prospect, supplier, person who calls or drops into your location, etc. Treat, and have each employee treat, every person they speak to or see as if it were Valentine's Day each day and the other person was the most important person in their life. I believe by transacting business in this way, great things will happen in your business such as: heightened productivity, greater efficiency, increased sales, greater understanding, improved morale, less stress, less absenteeism, less sickness and more joy and cooperation in the workplace. Your business will create greater value causing sales to soar.

God is providing us with opportunities to get back to basics – which is to exhibit love in all relationships. I believe the fruit of unconditional love in business relationships is money.

I believe this recession and all the unemployment is telling us to get back to love and relationships in business and when you maintain that focus within and outside the business (all stakeholders), your opportunity to succeed and win is greatly enhanced. Recall the old Fram Oil Filter TV commercial of the 70s? Its theme was, "pay me now or pay me later." In other words, an ounce of romance can produce a pound of rewards.

What or who are the important relationships in your life? In the December 2009 issue of Success Magazine, publisher, Darren Hardy, tells a story in his publisher's letter about visiting a man who was on his death bed. As Darren was leaving, the sick man grabbed his arm and said "Don't miss the point like I did. I wish I had spent as much time and energy accumulating relationships as I had houses. I wish I had invested my heart as aggressively as I did my money. Only now do I understand true wealth, and none of it appears on a balance sheet."[21]

As you look back on your life, will your relationships be what matters most? Does your life truly reflect this wisdom? How would you respond if I were to ask what your highest priorities are? Would you say, "Relationships with family and friends?" Would this answer be easily verified by looking at your calendar?

---

[21] *Success*, December 1009, p. 6

Michael Pink in his book, "Selling Among Wolves", **http://www.sellingamongwolves.com/** provides a fascinating discussion of how the Ten Commandments, as a relational guide, can have tremendous ramifications in your business helping to create sales and thus cash flow.

God made humans with certain motivational needs. When you and your personnel recognize these needs in all your stakeholders and speak to and serve those needs, which include: significance, authority, honor, peace of mind, security, love and acceptance, the need to be understood, and contentment, within the context of your product and or service, then you will be increasing the value you serve to your customers. You will actually be able to increase the level of cooperation you receive from your customers and employees.

You might be asking, "How does all this love and relationship talk work out in practice in my business?" Ask yourself the question, "What is it that my company needs most?" Maybe it is money, profits, sales, cash flow, liquidation of inventory or payment of accounts receivable. Each of these items, or others you might think of, directly or indirectly affects people and thus relationships. I once read, "We change when the pain of changing is less than the pain of staying where we are or staying the same." It might be time to consider a change, putting more time, energy, emphasis and focus on the relationships in your business.

Following are several strategies for success in relationships for you and your employees:

♥ Follow your natural instincts. Many companies fail to acknowledge and incorporate employees' strengths, gifts and design to maximize productivity and efficiency. For example, one company hired an accounting-type person who was good at and greatly enjoyed performing detailed and specific analytical work. However, the employee was assigned to make outside sales calls, prepare detailed written reports and then make oral presentations before a room full of peers. Because these things were very much outside of his comfort zone, area of interest and natural design, the employee experienced much anxiety and stress resulting in health issues.

The following points were taken from an article by Jeannine Aversa, AP Economics Writer, on Tuesday January 5, 2010:

- According to a new survey, only 45% of Americans are satisfied with their work. That was the lowest level ever recorded by the Conference Board research group in more than 22 years of studying the issue.
- Fewer workers consider their jobs to be interesting.
- There is no sense of teamwork in most places anymore.
- Workers who find their jobs uninteresting are less inclined to be innovative and take fewer calculated risks and less initiative resulting in decreased productivity contributing to reduced economic growth.
- 49% of workers say they are dissatisfied with their boss. That's up from 40% two decades ago.
- Many surveyed said they wish bosses would take time to listen to workers' ideas -- and their difficulties on the job.

Contrast the above examples with a story I recently heard from the owner of a business who received a shipment from a driver. The business owner asked the driver if he liked his job.

His response was, "I love my job".

"Why?" asked the business owner.

"I get to do what I love and what I feel I'm good at and what I feel best helps the company I work for. My company recognizes and acknowledges my strengths and their value to the overall operation. Adding to my enjoyment is the fact that all other employees are just like me. They are doing what they enjoy and are gifted in. Plus, when I make a delivery, like to you today, I know that the order is right because others in the company that touched this order did their job right and I won't have to take flak because someone made a mistake."

That is both job satisfaction and efficiency on the job!

♥ **Practice attention management**. Pay attention and be sensitive to what is going on with others. Part of serving others is what I call 'JIT' (just in time) relationship – giving people what they need at that moment, which is part of *relationship econo*mics – the art of connecting. This doesn't require special skills or training. Give people what you can simply and easily give away – the gift of attention, acceptance and respect. The ability to notice others, ask good questions to stimulate interest and really listen is highly valuable in developing and maintaining relationships. When these simple, doable things are done, you will find you have just constructed a simple 'on ramp to their heart.'

Jesus said in Matthew 6:21, "Where your treasure is, there your heart will be also." (NAS) What we treasure determines where we put or who gets our heart. People will invest in people, services and products they trust and trust is an investment of the heart. Where people will invest their heart, they will feel comfortable investing their money, loyalty and desire to have a long-term relationship. In front of that employee customer or supplier try putting a "♥" instead of a "$". Try doing your business with love and the money will follow.

♥ **Take risks**. When you love someone you take risks to do things for them. Here I am using the definition of risk to mean investing in the possibility or probability of a positive mutual outcome.

♥ **Put ego in place**. Philippians 2:3 – "Do nothing from selfishness or empty conceit, but with humility of mind let each of you regard one another as more important than himself." (NAS)

♥ **Continue to push the envelope**. Learn and practice the rule of 10%. It takes only a 10% improvement on an old product or service to make it a new product or service. Find and develop ways to improve what you are doing, for and with people, to harvest an incredible payoff. I've found that most employees know to some degree what their specific job requirements and responsibilities are, but really don't know *how* what they do contributes to the business. Often it has not been explained to them exactly what the business does for its customers. Once they understand and feel their contributions to the whole are valued and appreciated, they will enthusiastically provide ideas for improvement and growth.

Soliciting comments and recommendations from customers can open the door to vast possibilities. Galatians 5:13 says, "...through love serve one another." (NAS) Success begins with people.

♥ **Change your way of looking at the competition**. In the 2004 Olympic, Michael Phelps entered the games with the possibility of breaking Mark Spitz's record of seven medals. He had the opportunity to get eight. Phelps had just beaten his US teammate, Ian Crocker, in the butterfly by $1/100^{th}$ of a second and they were being interviewed about the event. In contrast to talking about their individual efforts, all they talked about was the team and about how genuinely happy they were for each other.

Unlike the strutting showboat egotism of some American athletes in other events, Phelps and Crocker unpretentiously shared the glory and the limelight. Within an hour of this interview it was announced that Phelps would step aside and let Crocker swim the upcoming 400 meter relay. Phelps, though having every right to swim in the event, allowed Crocker to take his place because he felt Crocker was the better swimmer in this event and he wanted to make sure the team won. Phelps' deferral to Crocker made headlines precisely because such an example of a Good Samaritan is so rare.

In a world filled with thoughts and business practices based on scarcity and competition, how do you compete day in and day out in your business?

I personally look to Nature, more specifically, the rainforest, as a model to guide my business. Bill Shireman, one of American's leading environmental advocates and CEO of the Future 500, and Tachi Kiuchi, former chairman and CEO of Mitsubishi Electric America, visited a number of rainforests in their quest to discover how business can profit from nature. Man's mindset has historically been to take resources from nature to make products to sell. Shireman and Kiuchi discovered the real profit from nature is the *wisdom* embedded there - principles found to cultivate more profitable businesses - rather than continue to extract physical resources from the rainforests.

They discovered how little direct competition there really was in the rainforest. They found a vast array of species, working interdependently with one another, cooperating as if for one another's success and viability (Does this sound like your industry?) The most valuable resources found in the rainforest were not the trees or other physical resources, but the relationships.

Species, though different from one another, like employees, each fulfilled their specific role or design. They found in the rainforest limits were positive forces, leading to innovation, bringing about change and initiating net gain or profit. The key was the various designs of different species. Each species, though uniquely different, cooperated with other species using their individual and unique design to produce value. Value, leading to net gain or profit, was achieved as combinations were brought together, creating synergy.

Put in a different context, many problems experienced in business today, I believe, are the result of an *orphan*

168

spirit in the workplace as well as the lack of a true godly, supernatural *fathering spirit*. Where the orphan spirit exists and the fathering spirit is absent, relationships disintegrate. Recall that relationships are at the core of any business.

This fathering spirit is characterized by unconditional love, exhibited by our Heavenly Father, Himself, as He gave freely His son, Jesus, to redeem and fully accept mankind. This highly desired spirit needed and wanted in the workplace is contrasted by what is mostly seen and exhibited today – a heart that is self-centered, self-absorbed, and self-serving The fatherless spirit exists when business owners, executives, supervisors and managers 'abandon' those under their charge in the workplace by focusing and centering on their own needs and desires at the expense of others.

The lack of a true, godly, supernatural fathering spirit promotes the orphan spirit in the workplace. Several characteristics of the orphan spirit usually witnessed in the workplace are:

- Obsession with self
- Inaccurate perception of the value of both themselves and others
- Compulsive drive to succeed at all costs
- Insecurity accompanied by the need to control others
- Inability to handle rejection properly, feeling they deserve to be and will be rejected by others.
- Critical, judgmental spirit
- Uncontrollable anger

Several root words describing the fathering spirit are: nourisher, protector, upholder, comforter, exhorter, one called to another's side, aid and advocate.

It is my opinion that for many years the most valuable asset in any organization – the employees - have been reappraised downward or devalued by owners, executive management, supervisors and managers lacking the fathering spirit. I believe God is telling us that one of the ways to improve the economy and individual businesses is to unleash the 'fathering spirit' in each business and to romance all relationships in the business. This is truly the **stimulus package** each business and the economy needs.

Try loving the competition! This last thought might be the greatest challenge to business thinking today. Respect and appreciate they also have a unique design that deserves to be valued and put into service.

I acknowledge that not everyone a business comes in contact with and romances is saleable or will become a customer. I also acknowledge that romancing employee relationships will not always lead to the results you might desire as competency is a big issue when it comes to employees. However, many such issues are beyond the scope of this book. My intent was to make you aware and alert to the benefits of romancing all relationships as a way of life.

What really does make the world go around? It's people and LOVE. Without either we would not have a world.

I love titles to books and music, and it's amazing how true some titles are and you really don't need to hear the song or read the book to get the true message. There's an old song from the early 80s by a group called the Motels titled, "Take the L out of Lover and its OVER". This song title is absolutely true as it relates to Romancing the Loan. Without being or playing the lover in relationships, even to your lender, it will truly be OVER!

At times our own light goes out, and is rekindled by a spark from another person. Each of us has cause to think with deep gratitude of those who have lighted the flame within us. Albert Schweitzer.

What act of kindness can you do today to light up someone's life? A candle that lights another loses no power!

"YES" FACTORS

- **Practice *relationship economics***

- **Love your neighbor (lender, employees, customers, competition)**

- **Employ *attention management***

- **Unique design is where value lies**

Appendix A

Lending Tool Kit/Forms

Following are three forms that are included for your review and use as you present your request to a lender. On my website *www.upyourbusiness.biz* I have these specific forms and others that can be downloaded. At a minimum these forms will give you a clearer idea as to the type of information a lender will want to receive.

In some instances lenders have their own forms. Don't hesitate to request specific forms they want you to use which will save both of you time. For example, many lenders have their own personal financial statement form (template) and personal cash flow statement. Some lenders do not have specific business loan forms aside possibly from an application form. Be prepared to put the information in your own format or use what I've provided on my website.

All lenders have a **Loan Request/Approval Form** similar to the one following that is used for their internal purposes. Provided as the first document they receive in your loan request package, this form will give the lender information in the language and format they are accustomed to viewing.

The **Borrower Loan Request Summary** is one I recommend be filled out as completely as possible. As a lender, I found it useful, and was always grateful to receive this information in the borrower's own words. This form provides the lender with more detailed information, mostly in narrative form, regarding your request, your business and financial history and your industry, etc. needed to complete their paperwork and process your request. Because you know better than anyone your company, your industry, your strengths and weaknesses as well as the risks and how they are mitigated, taking the initiative to provide in detail the information on the form allows you to "think for the lender " and gives you the voice in the loan proposal.

Sending the information via an email allowing the lender to 'cut and paste' the information into the loan presentation saves time leading to a speedier loan decision, which, of course, is what you want.

CHECKLIST FOR BUSINESS PURPOSE LOANS
Application

- ❏ Business Loan Request Form
- ❏ Financial Statements (3 yrs.) on Borrower(s)
- ❏ Interim Financial Statement on Borrowers(s)
- ❏ Tax Returns on Borrower(s) (3 years)
- ❏ Business Debt Schedule on Borrower(s)
- ❏ Business Plan
- ❏ Business Cash Flow Projections
- ❏ Personal Financial Statement on Guarantor(s)
- ❏ Personal Cash Flow Analysis
- ❏ Guarantor(s) Tax Returns (3 years)
- ❏ Management Resumes highlighting experience

Income Producing Real Estate Loans
(In addition to above)

- ❏ Executive Summary Template for Income Producing Real Estate Loans
- ❏ Rent Roll
- ❏ Operating Statements (last 3 years and current interim)
- ❏ Market Information/Characteristics
- ❏ Copy of Lease
- ❏ Property Description/Valuation Support
- ❏ Plans for Property/Capital Expenditure Budget

Miscellaneous

- ❏ Cash Flow Analysis (for Term Loan purposes)
- ❏ Liquidity Analysis (Cash Conversion Cycle)
- ❏ Working Capital Loan Collateral Summary (A/R, Inventory)
- ❏ Breakeven, DCR, Interest Rate Sensitivity Analysis
- ❏ Appraisal or Valuation Basis for Loans on Fixed Assets
- ❏ Insurance Binder or Certificate on Fixed Assets
- ❏ Accounts Receivable/Payable Aging for LOC
- ❏ Inventory Summary Report for LOC
- ❏ Borrowing Base Report (A/R, Inventory LOC)
- ❏ Authorization for Release of Information for Credit Check
- ❏ Request for Copy of Tax Return – Form 4506

LOAN REQUEST FORM

LOAN REQUEST FORM

DATE [   ]

CUSTOMER INFORMATION
BORROWER (S) _____
ADDRESS _____
CITY / STATE _____

GUARANTOR _____ TYPE OF GTY. _____ OWNER-SH %

TYPE OF BUSINESS _____
LEGAL FORM _____

BORROWER'S LOAN REQUEST:

#	Facility Type	Amount	Outstandings	Rate	Fees	Maturity	Terms	New/Renewal	Account #
1									
2									
3									
4									
5									

PURPOSE:

1	
2	
3	

COLLATERAL: (This request only. Cross-collateralized loans to remain open and secured with this collateral should be listed under "1st Mtg. Balance" section)

#	Description	Valuation Source	Appraiser & Date	Purchase Price	Gross Value	Eligible Value	Adv. Rate	Margined Value	1st Mtg. Holder	1st Mtg. Balance
								$ -		
								$ -		
								$ -		
								$ -		
Totals					$0	$0	$0	$0		

Total Collateral Value - This Request	$0
Total Collateral Value - Existing Debt	#REF!
Total Collateral Value - All Debt	#REF!

Cross Collateralized ○ YES ○ NO
Cross Defaulted ○ YES ○ NO

DEPOSIT RELATIONSHIP:

Name	Account #	Type	Date Opened	Current Balance	Avg. YTD Balance	NSF - YTD (#)
TOTAL DEPOSITORY ACCOUNTS				$0	$0	

EXPOSURE SUMMARY:

TOTAL DIRECT EXPOSURE (including addendum, if applicable)	$0.00
TOTAL INDIRECT EXPOSURE (including addendum, if applicable)	$0.00
THIS REQUEST	$0.00
TOTAL RELATIONSHIP EXPOSURE ("TRE")	$0.00

PRIMARY SOURCE OF REPAYMENT

SECONDARY SOURCE OF REPAYMENT

FINANCIAL INFORMATION:

BALANCE SHEET   Statement Date ___   Type ___

ASSETS		LIABILITIES		INCOME STATEMENT	
Cash		Accts. Payable		Sales	
Accts. Receivable		Payrolls		Cost of Sales	
Equipment		Notes Payable		Gross Profit	
Inventory		Mortgages		Depreciation Exp.	
Real Estate		Total Liabilities		Interest Expense	
Total Assets		Net Worth	$0	Total Expenses	
				Net Income	
				Debt Coverage Ratio	

PERSONAL FINANCIAL STATEMENT Statement Date ___

		CASH FLOW ANALYSIS		CBI REPORT		
Current Assets		Monthly Income		Name	Date	Beacon
Total Assets		Less:				
Total Liabilities		Monthly Expenses				
Net Worth	$0	Remaining Income	$0.00			
Outside N/W		Debt to Income Ratio				
Annual Income						

☐

BORROWER LOAN REQUEST SUMMARY

Borrower's Name: **Date:**

Request/Structure:
- Purpose
- How funds will be used/What goal will they achieve
- Sources of repayment
- Term
- Amortization
- Rate
- Method of handling funds disbursement (if applicable)
- Exceptions to loan policy (if applicable)
- Loan monitoring requirements (if applicable)

Existing Lender/Banking Relationship Summary:

Background/History of Business:

Industry History/Analysis:

Collateral Information:
Description   Value   Basis
Basis for Value – (attach)

Collateral Release Provision: (if applicable)

Management Capability/Character:

Historical Financial Results and Cash Flow Analysis:

Existing Debt: (with this lender)

Guarantors:

Strengths:

Weaknesses:

Risks/Mitigation:

Summary: Overriding factors/Cash/Liquidity/Guarantors

Appendix B

Why Coaching?

I grew up fairly adept at sports. First there was baseball, then football and golf. Very early in my sports career, my father, who played semi-pro baseball, contacted a former player who was a pitcher and coaxed him into coaching me on the physical and mental aspects of pitching. At that time and at my age, having an individual coach was rarely heard of or done. The progress I made simply by having someone work with, critique and help me with the mental process of pitching, was astounding and my improvement was noticeable. The value of what he taught me, especially the mental aspect, has served me well since then in sports, business, relationships and raising three children.

Many times during my sports career, especially in football, I tried to train and get into shape by myself. In preparation for the beginning of each new season, as hard as I tried on my own, I could not get into the kind of shape that I needed and wanted to be in to play in a game. A coach could encourage and push me beyond my perceived limitations where I discovered real growth and strength could be developed.

Early in my golf career (junior high and high school) I tried to learn, practice and improve by myself. I would watch the pros on TV and then during practice try to imitate their actions. I cut out magazines articles, put them in a binder and read them regularly. However, nothing had the impact on my game as much as getting a lesson from the pro (coach) at the club where I grew up playing. I could tell him where I was having trouble and he always had the perfect answer. He knew my swing, its strengths, weaknesses and tendencies and could give me advice to go work out the problems. I recently signed up to play in a charity golf tournament and although I hadn't played or practiced in eight months, while playing the tournament, I recalled some of those lessons I received during my early years of golf which enabled me to look like I knew what I was doing.

While a young loan officer in Houston, Texas, the economy was flourishing and we were getting a lot of loan requests from many different types of contractors. After making a presentation for a loan to a contractor that was denied, the head of the loan committee asked me if we could talk. He offered to go over what he had learned during his career about this very specialized area of lending. He made the time to coach me and by listening to and applying the truths he taught, it saved me countless problems over the next twenty-five years of my career.

I was with another bank and we knew there were problems with the progress we were making in our market place. The president of the bank endorsed my suggestion of testing the bank management to indicate our individual strengths and weaknesses and evaluating these new found results in relation to the bank's goals and subsequently, using the information discovered for a team building exercise.

We discovered many helpful and interesting facts about ourselves, corporately as well as individually. The most startling and eye-opening discovery was that all but one of the fifteen individuals on the management team were 'starters' and only one was deemed to be a 'finisher'. Once this fact was revealed during the team building exercise, we all knew what one of our major problems was in our attempt to accomplish our goals; we needed someone to keep us on track, like a coach would in athletics.

Business is a life enriching sport. Like any game sport, you can go through the frequently frustrating, sometimes discouraging and often humbling process of figuring things out yourself, spending precious time and energy. Or you can engage someone who can pinpoint your strengths and help you maximize them, come along side you to identify your best opportunities, help you avoid pitfalls, assist you in expanding your network and your market and help you to find the balance of work with the rest of your life.

The following short story is true and it's mine.

I walked out of my client's office one evening shaking my head. A full year before, I had suggested ways that might help to save his company, if applied. Didn't he know, as many of his counter parts in Texas did in the mid 80s, that unless he did some specific things, his business might die as thousands had already done during this oil and gas and real estate bust? I was trying to do my job, yet being mindful of lender liability, I had to be careful and not dictate to him what he had to do; this was no time to be sued. Never, in my 20 years of commercial lending, had I seen so many business owners and professionals do and say things to protect themselves in such dire economic times. This CEO and his business were in trouble and he knew it, yet he didn't know what to do. He, like many in Texas during the mid 80s, had no prior experience of going through a financial storm such as this. He was also fearful for his business and family and his 50 employees and their families. I was almost as frustrated as this business owner. I wanted so desperately to help, but didn't seem to be helping.

The CEO hired me as his banker and lender because I had been recommended by a mutual friend, who had been my customer for many years. We had similar values and I caught the vision he had for his company and believed in what he was doing. Over time I refinanced his loans and in the ensuing months I spent considerable time with him monitoring the progress of his business, suggesting varying courses of action and providing guidance from a classic lender's point of view. I was sincere, and what I was telling the CEO was valuable, correct and proven information. But nothing happened!

Then I realized that being the forceful, demanding banker, as I had witnessed my whole career and had been taught by my managers, was not right. But wait, wasn't it true that "he who had the gold rules?" Weren't the business owners supposed to listen and obey?

In many ways, I stopped being a traditional banker/lender that night.

My role shifted that fateful night from being the answer man to becoming a coach and partner to the business owner, helping him/her discover what is needed and identify and remove barriers to moving forward.

Getting to the Heart of Business

Over the next few months, I began a search into my own life purposes, my skills and talents, and how I might provide greater value to my customers. I learned that there is never a lack of value in the marketplace. Value is value and as long as there are people living on this planet, there will be things and services they value. If a business serves itself – lives to only perpetuate itself – it will certainly die. But if the purpose and function of a business is to continually discover and provide value for others, then it is impervious to economic pitfalls and has no real competition.

In this process I discovered what I call my true asset which I define as that unique quality or gift that is truly me, and when applied properly, always provides value. When my true asset meets the need of another, they in turn are willing to exchange something they have that is of value to me, usually currency. I'd like to share with you what I have learned:

Business is All About Relationships

I love the people who lead businesses. Having spent my life working with and serving business owners, I understand some of the pressures they face. I've witnessed the risks of success and failure and seen the results of the temptations to compromise. I've heard their terrors of worry in the middle of the night over their business, their families and the customers they were losing or missing.

Discovering my true asset, which is listening to, understanding, supporting and encouraging others, enabled me as a business lender to add value to the people God called me to serve.

My prevailing passion during my work life has been to help business owners grow in their ability to manage and improve their businesses. Through my coaching business, Up Your Business, I offer a variety of options to help you enter or maintain your personal path to mastery and to increasingly improve revenues, profit and personal fulfillment in your business.

Questions Unleash Power

No matter how much I know, or how right I am, people learn when they're ready. Giving my clients answers may not promote the right kind of change. Questions stimulate thinking. They engage and penetrate the hardened places in our life. Questions can disrupt and may bring about or cause pain to surface. Just like in our bodies, pain and inflammation are signs that something needs to change. When confronted with a question our brain goes to work and focuses its considerable energy on working out the answer.

Jesus led his disciples with questions and rebuked the Pharisees with questions. I reasoned that if I was to be more effective in helping CEO's make the necessary changes for their businesses, I had to ask the right questions.

A consultant is an 'answer man', but a coach serves by prompting and leading. As a coach, my goal is to empower the business owner by asking questions to help her/him uncover root causes, discover options, own contributions to the problem, choose priorities and commit to actions. There is a moment when (s)he is ready to hear, to answer questions honestly, and to embrace change. It's in those moments that I must be patient, sensitive and seek to understand what is happening in the business owner's life and business. Coaching is a process that involves change and development both for the business owner **and** for me. We enter into a partnership that removes obstacles, finds solutions and moves forward with ease.

A Fulfilling Journey

Coaching CEO's and business owners one-on-one in a way that both challenge and encourages them is demanding and requires me to keep growing. It is also a very fulfilling way to accomplish my vision of helping the people I've been called to serve. My success as a coach comes from a passion to partner with you, the entrepreneurs and business owners, to help you enjoy the fruits of achieving your potential. By using my ability to use targeted questions to get a clear picture of you and your business and applying intuition, business intelligence and tenacity in turning problems into solutions, I am able to help business owners understand and stay on their path to mastery, to rapidly grow and to increasingly improve revenue, profit and personal fulfillment.

SERVICES

Coaching/Advisory Services

My goal is to position you to confidently apply for or seek renewal of a loan and build a solid bridge of communication between you and your lender(s). The steps to achieving this include:

1. Identify problems and wants.

2. Develop a strategic approach to take you from your wants to their fulfillment.

3. Assist you in putting together documentation required by the lender.

4. Learn the lender's language and mindset.

5. Apply for and support a loan request.

6. Follow up after the request to see that the loan is closed efficiently and quickly.

Consulting

1. Work side by side with you and your personnel to physically prepare a loan package and verbal presentation to your lender.

2. Strengthen your business with proactive cash flow intelligence support.

3. Provide a risk assessment to strengthen your company's risk management process and raise the risk intelligence of your team.

4. Analyze and evaluate the risk and return of the investment in physical assets.

Representation

Represent you and your business, either with you and other team members or by myself to present your loan request or negotiate for you with the lender. Periodically represent you and your business with your lender to maintain an open and productive level of communication.

Maintenance

Set up and provide you with a schedule to assist in meeting all reporting requirements and or loan covenants in a timely and professional manner. The goal is to ensure the positive relationship with your lender(s) garnered in the loan presentation and approval process isn't lost during the loan payment period.

Speaking

Provide seminars, workshops and keynote presentations to professional groups, franchises, associations, clubs and high school and college students on a variety of business leadership, banking and inspirational topics including:

- Romancing the Loan -14 principles to help your lender open the vault to you

- Tapping into your businesses' most valuable asset – your cash flow

- Business wealth secrets from the planet's most successful business model

- Entrepreneurial Thinking

- Tapping the strengths of your strongest resource, your employees

- Taking the Competition Out of Business

To implement a coaching program for you and your business, contact

www.larry@upyourbusiness.biz

or web site: www.upyourbusiness.biz

or call 828-371-3436.

> "The value of a man should be seen in what he gives and not in what he is able to receive - Albert Einstein

Up Your Business Coaching

Features Benefits Value Chart

Features "We have..."	Benefits "It will..."	Value "Which means..."
Ability to speak the lender's language	Improve communication	Better teamwork Improved morale Increased productivity
Company sponsored training program	Overcome anxiety and fear of preparing data	Self confidence Improved image
Turn key loan package	Faster response from lender	Peace of mind Fewer surprises
Experience in working with lenders	Allow you to continue to do what you do best	No disruption or loss of productivity
Ability to think for the Lender	Provide the Lender with what they need and want	Simplifies, shortens the process Makes you look good
Ability to represent you with the Lender	Reduces possible conflicts	Effective communication
Ability to know what the Lender wants/needs	Save time, effort and energy	Less stress and anxiety
Ability to help you with your Vision	Provide clarity for your company	Improved probability of getting the loan requested
Experienced former commercial lenders working on your behalf	Enhance your ability to receive a YES	Increased ROI
Understanding of the loan application process	Provides peace of mind	Less stress and worry
Experienced underwriter and analyst on staff	Meet Lenders needs	Giving the Lender what they want to see
Loan packaging plans	You look professional	Gives peace of mind
Help build strong relationships with Lenders	Improve your status and favor with the Lender	Receiving what you want and need from your Lender

Appendix C

Resources

I believe Eric Hoffer's insight is now more relative than ever, "In a time of drastic change, it is the learner who inherits the future. The learned (experts) usually find themselves equipped to live in a world that no longer exists." As things continue to rapidly change in our world, it is more and more imperative that you be a learner. You must be willing to look for and accept change to achieve your goals and dreams.

I love the following poem and feel that it speaks well to being a learner:

"How to Change the World"
Written on a tomb in Westminster Abbey

When I was young and free and my imagination had no limits, I dreamed of changing the world.

As I grew older and wiser I discovered the world would not change

So I shortened my sights somewhat and decided to change only my country,

But it too seemed unmovable.

As I grew into my twilight years, in one last desperate attempt,

I settled for changing only my family, those closest to me,

But alas, they would have none of it.

And now I realize as I lie on my death bed, if I had only changed myself first,

Then by example I might have changed my family,

From their inspiration and encouragement I would have been able to better my country,

And who knows, I might have even changed the world.

Anthony Robbins said, "Success leaves clues." I love that saying because it is so true! Almost everything you want to do has already been done by someone else. People have left clues to success in books, manuals, videos, tapes, CDs, courses, seminars in college and trade schools and, even more importantly, in their memories. Most of us could exceed even our wildest dreams if we would take advantage of what is available to help us get from where we currently are to where we want to be.

Jack Canfield, in his book "The Success Principles", mentions three ways to find clues:

- Seek out a teacher, coach, mentor, a manual, book, audio program or internet resource
- Seek out someone who has already done what you want to do
- Ask someone if you can shadow them for a day and watch them work

Notes

Introduction

1. Leonard , *Summoned to Lead,* (Grand Rapids, Michican: Zondervan, 2004), 24. - p. 153
2. Matthew 22:37-40 p. 29
3. Jeremiah 29:11 p. 32

Chapter 1

1. BrainyQuote.com "Andrew Carnegie Quotes," p. 34
   http://www.brainyquote.com/quotes/authors/a/andrewcarnegie.html
2. http://ericjeffersonbeck.com/?p=847   p. 35
3. http://ericjerrersonbeck.com/?p=847   p. 35
4. Goodreads.com, "quotes by Brian Tracy", - p. 41
   http://www.goodreads.com/author/quotes/22033.Brian_Tracy
5. Proverbs 22:7   p. 42
6. Galatians 4:1 p. 42

Chapter 2

1. 1 Corinthians 16:14 p. 46
2. Philippians 4:8 p. 55
3. 1 Timothy 2:1 p. 56

Chapter 3

1. Bachrach, Bill, *Values Based Selling,* (San Diego, California: Aim High Publishing, 1996)   p. 60
2. 2 Corinthians 6:14 p. 67

Chapter 4

1. Gitomer, Jeffrey, *Little Black Book of Connections,* (Austin, Texas: Brad Press, 2006), front fly page. - p. 69
2. Abraham Maslow, "Theory of Human Motivation", 1943 – p.70
3. Philippians 2:3-4 p. 71
4. Jim Henderson, *a.k.a"Lost", Discovering Ways to Connect With The People Jesus Misses Most (Colorado Springs, Colorado:* Waterbrook Press, 2005) p.104.- p. 72
5. Psalm 119:72 p. 74
6. 2 Chronicles 1:8   p. 74
7. Matthew 19:16-22   p. 74

8. Harvey Mackay, *Dig Your Well Before Your're Thirsty,* (New York, NY: Doubleday, 1990). – p .75

Chapter 5

1. Gary Chapman, *The Five Love Languages,* (Chicago, IL: Northfield Publishing, 1992), p. 17. - p. 77
2. Kevin Davis, *Getting Into Your Customer's Head,* (New York, NY: Crown Business, 1996). p. 78
3. John Gray, *Men Are From Mars, Women Are From Venus*, (New York, NY: HarperCollins Publishers, 1993). p. 83

Chapter 7

1. QuoteDB.com" Brian Tracy," http://www.quotedb.com/quotes/2322 p. 95
2. Simplealogy News.com, - p.95 p/http://usmc359.mail.yahoo.com/mc/welcome?.9x=1&.tm=125011 85054&.rand=f1gi94aq1vc26#-
3. Michael Masterson, *Ready, Fire, Aim,* (Hokoken, NJ: John Wiley & Sons, 2008) p.196. - p. 97
4. Jack Canfield, Janet Switzer, *The Success Principles,* (New York, NY: HarperCollins Publishers Inc., 2005) p.99. *– p.97*
5. Michael Pink, *Rainforest Strategy*, (Lake Mary, Florida: Excel Books, 2008) p. 32. – p.99

Chapter 8

1. Al Ries, Jack Trout, *Positioning-The Battle For Your Mind,* (New York, NY: McGraw-Hill Inc., 1981) -p.102
2. USA Today, June 26, 2008, p.103 http://www.usatoday.com/life/movies/news/2008-06-26-will-smith_N.htm -
3. DeWittJones.com, "Seeing the Ordinary As Extraordinary", http://www.dewittjones.com/html/seeing_the_ordinary.shtml p. 104

Chapter 9

1. BrainyQuotes.com, "Zig Ziglar Quotes,"- p. 108 http://www.brainyquote.com/quotes/authors/z/zig_ziglar_2.html

Chapter 10

1. Philip Campbell, *Never Run Out of Cash,* (Tomball, TX: Grow and Succeed Publishing LLC, 2004) www.neverrunoutofcash.com, www.growandsucceed.com. p. 114

2. Habakkuk 2:7 p.116
3. Proverbs 22:7 p.117
4. Psalm 37:21 p. 117, 122
5. Deuteronomy 28:43-44 p. 120
6. Proverbs 22:26 p 121
7. James 4:13-15 p.121
8. Proverbs 22:1 p. 122
9. Romans 13:8 p 123

Chapter 12

1. Richard Koch, *The 80/20 Principle,* (New York, NY: Doubleday, 1998) p. 132

Chapter 13

1. St. Francis of Assisi quote, - p. 135
http://bible.org/seriespage/communication-skills
2. Shane Murphy, *Achievement Zone,* (New York, NY: G.P. Putnam's Sons) p.136
3. Romans 14:19   p. 137

Chapter 14

1. Nicholas Boothman, *How to Connect in Business in 90 Seconds or Less,* (New York, NY: Workman Publishing, 2002) p. 141
2. Jack Canfield, Janet Switzer, *The Success Principles,* (New York, NY: HarperCollins Publishers Inc., 2005) p.6-7 -   p. 142

Chapter 15

1. Leonard Sweet, *Summoned to Lead,* (Grand Rapids, Michigan: Zondervan, 2004) p. 153

Chapter 16

1. Genesis 1:27 - p.155
2. Matthew 22:37-40 – p. 156, 159
3. 1 Corinthians 13 – p.156
4. Tachi Kiuchi and Bill Shireman, *What We Learned in the Rainforest: Business Lessons from Nature,* (San Francisco, California: Berrett-Koehler Publishers, 2002) p. 9   - p.157,168
5. John Wooden and Steve Jamison, *"Wooden on Leadership",* (New York, NY: McGraw-Hill Companies, 2005) p. 158
6. Proverbs 27:23-24 p. 158
7. Luke 10:30-37 p. 159
8. *Success*, December 1009, p. 6   p. 162

9. Michael Q. Pink, *Selling Among Wolves,* (Gainesville, Florida: Bridge-Logos, 2000). p. 163
10. Jeannine Aversa, AP Economics Writer, p. 164 http://dailyreporter.com/blog/2010/01/05/americans-job-satisfaction-falls-to-record-low-706-am-1510/
11. Matthew 6:21 p. 166
12. Philippians 2:3, p.166
13. Galatians 5:13 p. 167

INDEX

www.ingramcontent.com/pod-product-compliance
Lightning Source LLC
Chambersburg PA
CBHW031932190326
41519CB00007B/500